A WARTIME JOURNEY

FROM LEWIS RUN, PA TO GERMANY AND BACK

World War II Combat Experiences of Staff Sergeant
Nataline Piscitelli, U.S. Army US13048909

Tank Commander with the U.S. 2nd Armored Division

"Hell on Wheels" in Western Europe
(May 30, 1944 to September 30, 1945)

PREPARED BY HIS NEPHEW
COLONEL ALBERT C. COSTANZO
U.S. ARMY (RETIRED)

ISBN: 978-1-7348602-0-7 (paperback)
       978-1-7348602-1-4 (ebook)

IN APPRECIATION to
BILL MAULDIN
STAHLER
THE ORANGE POST. 1943

Image copyright© Estate of William Mauldin.
Courtesy of Fantagraphics Books.

NOTE: *This story was reviewed and completed in 2019 by Nat's daughter, Peggy Anne, after the death of Albert.*

Book cover and interior design by TeaBerryCreative.com

STAFF SERGEANT NATALINE ANTHONY PISCITELLI
COMPANY E, 2ND BATTALION, 66TH ARMORED REGIMENT
2ND ARMORED DIVISION, "HELL ON WHEELS"
FEBRUARY 10, 1942 – OCTOBER 21, 1945

TABLE OF CONTENTS

FOREWORD

I have read many books about World War II (WWII), its battles, and those who fought them. Being a career Army officer, I was intrigued by the strategy of the war. At the Piscitelli 50th Anniversary Reunion in 1997, I had the opportunity to sit and talk with Uncle Nat about his WWII experiences. He was more than willing to share them with me. He recalled events that even his own family didn't know about. I was glad to listen to him and even happier to write about them.

> *(Note: I grew up calling my Uncle by his childhood nickname of "Naz." However, when he enlisted, he was known as "Nat" or "Nate"—the name now used by his wife, his immediate family, and his friends in California. In this book, I will refer to him as "Nat," though his WWII letters back home are signed as "Naz.")*

Until I interviewed Uncle Nat and other veterans who were involved in some of these battles, a completely different story, one more "true to life," emerged. Now I could visualize what

General Eisenhower meant when he said: "More importantly even than the weapons, however, was the indomitable fighting spirit of the men of the Allied nations who wielded them. The courage and devotion to duty which they exhibited throughout the campaign, in the grim days of the Ardennes counteroffensive as well as in the excitement of the dash across France and, later, the advances into the midst of Germany, were unsurpassable. It is the spirit that had enabled them to withstand the shocks of Dunkirk and Pearl Harbor which brought us at last to Lubeck, to Torgau, and to Berchtesgaden."

Uncle Nat served in Europe in 1944–1945 with the 2nd Armored Division ("Hell on Wheels") as it fought across France, Belgium, Holland, and Germany. Therefore, I prepared this account of his actions as a tribute, not only to him but to those veterans who had similar experiences. I not only want to tell his story, but I want to tell it as he and other U.S. soldiers saw and lived it while engaging the Germans in deadly combat.

"You'll get over it, Joe. Once I was
ina write a book exposin' the Army after th' war myself."

IMAGE COPYRIGHT© ESTATE OF WILLIAM MAULDIN.
COURTESY OF FANTAGRAPHICS BOOKS.

How to relate Uncle Nat's story is best expressed by Bill
Mauldin in his WWII cartoons and writings featuring "Willie
and Joe" in his book, *Up Front*, which is referenced in this book.

Bill Mauldin drew "pictures of an army full of blunders and efficiency, irritations and comradeship. But, most of all, full of men who can fight a ruthless war against ruthless enemies, and still grin at themselves."

Bill Mauldin also went on to state in his book: "Often soldiers who are going home say they are going to tell the people how fortunate we were to stop the enemy before he was able to come and tear up our country. They are also going to tell the people that it is a pretty rough life over here. But no matter how much we try, we can never give the folks at home any idea of what war really is. I guess you must go through it to understand its horror. You can't understand it by reading magazines or newspapers or by looking at pictures or by going to newsreels. You have to smell it and feel it all around you until you can't imagine what it used to be like when you walked or tossed clubs up into horse chestnut trees or fished for perch or when you did anything at all without a pack, rifle, and a bunch of grenades. No war is easy for those who fight it."

I. REFLECTIONS

"There is an appointed time for everything, and a time for every affair under the heavens. A time to love, and a time to hate; a time of war, and a time of peace." (Ecclesiastes 3: Verses 1 and 8)

"The soldier above all other people prays for peace, for he must suffer and bear the deepest wounds and scars of war." (General Douglas MacArthur)

"At the core, the American citizen soldiers knew the difference between right and wrong, and they didn't want to live in a world in which wrong prevailed. So, they fought and won, and we, all of us, living and yet to be born, must be forever profoundly grateful." (Stephen E. Ambrose, *Citizen Soldiers*, p. 473)

"They answered the call to help save the world from the two [Germany and Japan] most powerful and ruthless military machines ever assembled, instruments of conquest in the hands of fascist maniacs. They faced great odds and a late start, but they did not protest. At a time in their lives when their days and nights should have been filled with innocent adventure, love, and the lessons of the workaday world, they were fighting, often hand to hand, in the most primitive conditions possible, across the bloodied landscape of France, Belgium, Italy, Austria. They fought their way up the necklace of South Pacific islands few had ever heard of before and made them a fixed part of American history--islands with names like Iwo Jima, Guadalcanal, Okinawa. They were in the air every day, in skies filled with terror, and they went to sea on hostile waters far removed from the shores of their homeland." (Tom Brokaw, *The Greatest Generation*, p. xix)

"They were not in the service for some limited tour of duty. They were in for 'the duration.' They understood that they could not go home and pick up the threads of their personal lives until the war was won. A generation of young Americans put their lives on the line, not because they wanted to be heroes, but because there was no alternative. And they did it with a typically American spirit…there is no mistaking the dedication and the bravery they displayed. These were gallant folk." (Charles Osgood, *Kilroy Was Here*, pp. xvii-xviii)

"They are very different now. Don't let anybody tell you they aren't. They need a lot of people speaking for them and telling about them—not speaking for fancy bonuses and extra privileges. You can't pay money for what they have done. They need people telling about them so that they will be taken back into their civilian lives and given a chance to be themselves again." (Bill Mauldin, *Up Front*, p. 8)

HOPE FOR TOMORROW
Dear God, we pray to You
For people in all the world,
For other nations,
For other races,
For people who think differently
And live differently.
Help us to respect, understand,
And love each other.
Let there be no hate among nations.
Forgive all injustice.
Let wars end.
Let Your message be
Proclaimed everywhere.
Give us peace. Amen

(*Salesian Missions Pamphlet #49727*, 2002)

II. INTRODUCTION

Nat grew up in Lewis Run, PA. It is a small borough with about 800 inhabitants nestled in the Allegheny Mountains in northwestern Pennsylvania. It is six miles south of Bradford, PA—once known as "The Oil Metropolis of the World" because of the many oil wells and oil pumps scattered on the mountainsides. It is surrounded by small towns with names like Cyclone, Big Shanty, Mount Alton, Lafayette, Kushequa, and Kinzua. The Lewis Run area is blessed to have mild springs, comfortable summers, and cool and colorful autumns. However, it is renowned for its severe winters. It is common for the area to have below zero temperatures and record high snowfalls. On many occasions, it is the coldest spot in the nation.

Most of Lewis Run's inhabitants are descendants of Italians, Slovaks, Irish, English, and Welsh immigrants who came to the area in the early 1900s. They traveled by train from New York City to Bradford—about 400 miles. They then made the short six-mile trip by horse and buggy on a dirt road to

Lewis Run. To provide for their families, they had to work and to work hard! The men and even some children worked in the wood cutting industry, in brick plants, or in the newly discovered oil fields. They were generally paid only one dollar for 12 hours of work. You can only admire this generation because they arrived in a country where there was no welfare system, no social security system, no unemployment pay, no Medicare or Medicaid, nor many other social benefits like we have today. They truly believed in the message conveyed when they saw the Statue of Liberty as they sailed into New York Harbor: "Give me your tired, your poor, your huddled masses yearning to breathe free."

> "Coming to this country as steerage passengers: penniless, uneducated in most cases, and perhaps friendless, it is a miracle that they made it all the way. Hiring out to do any job, no matter how menial or how long the hours, the solid citizens, many of whom never learned to speak English well, kept a roof overhead and raised their children. Supplementing their meager income with a little garden plus the wild fruits and greens of the field and mountains, the doughty Latins began to inch their way toward security." (*The Bradford Era,* March 1, 1976)

Families took care of family members with loving care and respect. Nearly every family had a garden in their backyard where they raised most of their vegetables and shared any extras with their friends and neighbors. They also picked buckets full of leeks, mushrooms, wild strawberries, blackberries, and red and black raspberries in the fields and woods around the town. They canned many jars of fruits and vegetables to carry them through the long winters. It was also common for them to raise their own dairy cows, chickens, and pigs. Twice a day you could see the cows on the main street as they were herded to and from the pastures in the hills. The clanging of the cowbells would echo through the valley. Each cow seemed to know when to peel off and go to its own barn. The pigs were slaughtered during the winter. Their squealing was heard throughout the town as they were killed. The hills were always alive with gunshots as the hunters in the town went to the hills to hunt rabbits, squirrels, woodchucks, raccoons, and especially deer. It was common in the town to see a dozen or more deer being dressed out on any given day during deer season.

Nat's parents were two of these immigrants. His father, Umberto (Humbert) Piscitelli, was born in Cervino, Italy on February 21, 1885. The surname "Piscitelli" means "one who is a good swimmer." On January 14, 1901, at the age of 15, he sailed from Naples, Italy on the SS Kaiser, arriving in New York City two weeks later to be with his father, Francesco Piscitelli. He then came to the Bradford, PA area where he took the "Americanized" name of "Albert Fresh" to give him a "fresh" start in this land of opportunity called "LaMerica." He became a naturalized United States citizen on February 12, 1926. He died on January 15, 1974, at the age of 89.

Nat's mother, Annina (Anna) Carrara, was born in Pettorano Sul Gizio, Italy on March 8, 1888. She came to the United States on April 28, 1904, at the age of 16, on the SS Germania to be with her parents. She also settled in Lewis Run. She and Humbert were married two years later on August 15, 1906, at St. Bernard's Church in Bradford, PA. Their marriage license application shows Humbert's name as "Albert Fresh." She became a naturalized United States citizen on May 23, 1941, and died on July 30, 1960, at the age of 72.

Humbert worked at the Hanley Brick Company in Lewis Run as a bricklayer for more than 50 years before retiring in 1956. The bricks were known throughout the world as "Bradford Reds." He liked to tell the story that, if he took two or three bricks home each night in his lunch pail, he would have had more than enough to build his house. However, he never did build that brick house even though he built brick homes for others in Lewis Run and Bradford.

Mealtime at the Piscitelli household was the highlight of anyone's visit. Anna was a great cook of Italian specialties, especially homemade spaghetti and meatballs. She normally made them for dinner on Thursday nights and Sunday afternoons.

Her meals were served in the traditional Italian style to emulate the colors of the Italian flag: green garden vegetables, white bread, cheese, and red tomato sauce. Her typical breakfast was fried potatoes and peppers. For lunch, she would serve you sandwiches made with Italian salami, capicola, cheese, fried peppers, and eggs. Nat's nephew, Tom Piscitelli, son of Nat's brother, Clem, remembers her meals this way:

> "Our summer family vacations were always in Lewis Run. We stayed at Grandpa and Grandma's. My earliest recollection is arriving very late, midnight or so, and the house was all lit up and full of people. We immediately sat down to the dining table and Grandma served us a full meal of pasta, vegetables, bread, and salad. I can still picture Grandma walking around the table, just a bowl cradled in one arm, serving pasta to everyone. It seemed like you'd take one bite and she'd give two back."

Natalino Anthony Piscitelli was born on December 25, 1919, in Lewis Run, PA. He was the ninth of 11 children and the fourth son of Humbert and Anna in their family of five sons and six daughters. Because he was born on Christmas Day, he was named "Natalino"—the Italian version of a male's name to commemorate the "Nativity." His brothers and sisters and their children call him by his nickname "Naz" or "Uncle Naz."

Nat attended grammar school from 1927-1935 in Lewis Run. His school was a two-story, four-room building for all eight grades. There were no inside bathroom facilities—only "two-holer" outhouses in the back of the school. There were neither preschool nor kindergarten classes in those days. One teacher taught two grades in each room. He was taught spelling, reading, writing, arithmetic, grammar, geography, history, and civics. Each day, students performed chores such as sweeping the wooden classroom floors with oil-soaked sawdust, emptying pencil sharpeners, erasing/washing blackboards, or dusting blackboard erasers. There were normally two recess periods, one in the morning and one in the afternoon on the school's playground covered with small rocks and some grass. He and the other students went home for lunch each day as there wasn't any cafeteria in this small school. He graduated from the Lewis Run Grade School in 1935, during the Great Depression (1929–1941).

He attended St. Bernard High School in Bradford from 1935-1939 in a class of only 39 students. There were no school buses, so he hitchhiked a ride to get back and forth to Bradford, some six miles from Lewis Run. His favorite teacher was Sister Naomi who taught bookkeeping. Every Monday, she had her students count the Sunday church collection. One time the class was short only one cent and went to Sister for help. She told the class, in no uncertain terms, to figure out this trivial shortage. One of the strictest nuns in the school was Sister

Victorine—a tall, awesome looking, no-nonsense nun—who insisted that everyone sit up straight in her English classes. He learned from all these nuns the true value of self-discipline and listening skills which helped him throughout his military and civilian careers.

He played an end position on the high school football team where he lettered in the sport before he injured his knee in 1938. He jokingly believes to this day that his school would have retired his Number 42 jersey if he had not been hurt. He was once having trouble with Math, but Sister Bernice gave him a passing grade of 75 so he could stay on the football team. He was one of six lettermen in his class. They all served in the U.S. Armed Forces in WWII. They saw action in Europe and the South Pacific. They all survived; however, Nat was wounded in Europe, Nick Camas suffered ear damage in the Philippines, and George Corignani's appendix burst while he was on a troopship bound for Europe. As of 2005, Nat was the only one living.

After graduating from high school, Nat worked, like his father, at the Hanley Brick Company in Lewis Run for seventy-five cents an hour. That was about the only place where a high school graduate living in the Bradford Area could find work during the last years of the Great Depression (1929–1941). He was assigned to a table where he sorted out the bad bricks from the good ones. His brother, Steve, was his boss, but he made only five cents more for eighty cents an hour. During WWII, the brick plant made curved, acid resistant bricks to line circular chemical tanks. The bricks were made for the Monsanto Corporation and were shipped to Russia in wooden crates packed with straw, fifty bricks to a crate. The plant also supplied some of the bricks to build the Rockefeller Center in New York City.

Nat grew up in an environment of large families whose lives revolved around work, relatives, and the sport for the season (softball, baseball, football, sledding, etc.). The young people organized most of their games without coaches, uniforms, or a liability insurance requirement like is done today. One of his favorite pastimes during the major league baseball season was to listen to "Rosey" Rowswell's broadcasts of the Pittsburgh Pirates games on radio station KDKA in Pittsburgh, PA. Whenever a player hit a home run, Rosey's favorite expression was: "Open your window Aunt Minnie and push your petunias aside because here she comes!"

In the late 1930s to early 1940s, Nat's brother-in-law, Crescenzo "Barb" Costanzo, and his family operated a small theater in Lewis Run adjoining Barb's barbershop. It was called the "Family Theatre." Movies were only shown on weekends and were 16-mm reruns of those first shown to the public one to two years earlier. Nat would sometimes help by selling movie tickets.

At that time, there were no street names in this small town. Everyone just knew where people lived. All the residents had box numbers assigned at the local post office in the middle of town. They went there twice a day, in the morning and late afternoon, to pick up their mail. The Piscitelli's box number was "91" and was used by Nat's oldest sister, Fannie, until her passing in 2007.

It seems that every guy in Lewis Run had a nickname that stuck with him for life, like "Nat," "Dizzy," "Lanky," "Bugs," "Lefty," "Clown," "Trix," "Hobo Jack," to mention a few. The young men were together for comradeship in the Boy Scouts or in "The Lewis Run Rangers." These were also the ones who either enlisted or were drafted into the Army, Navy, and Marine Corps or worked in defense plants to support the total war effort.

In Lewis Run alone, with a population of only 800, there were 134 men and women who served in WWII, most of whom were first-generation Americans. This is a very high percentage. Their names and branches of service are shown at the end of this book. Of the 134, eight were killed. It was common for many families to have more than one of their members serving in the armed forces. The DePrater family had six sons, and the Langianese and Pace families each had five sons who served in WWII. There were many families, like the Piscitelli's, who had three sons in the service. All 134 names were inscribed on an Honor Roll placed in the center of town. It was paid for by Mr. and Mrs. Peter Leone, who owned a grocery store and barroom in Lewis Run and had two sons in the service—Mike in the U.S. Army Air Corps in Oklahoma and Jim in the U.S. Marines in the South Pacific. The Honor Roll was placed in a yard on the town's main street next to Leone's Grocery Store.

General George S. Patton, Jr. expected this from these first-generation Americans as stated in his message to his troops before they invaded Sicily in July 1943:

> "When we land, we will meet German and Italian soldiers who it is our honor and privilege to attack and destroy. Many of you have in your veins German and Italian blood but remember that these ancestors of yours so loved freedom that they gave up home and country to cross the ocean in search of liberty. The ancestors of the people we shall kill lacked the courage to make such a sacrifice and remained as slaves." *(Underlines added.)* (Philip Gerard, *Secret Soldiers*, pp. 78-79)

In Volume III of *The Descendants of the Grilli and Carrara Families of Pettorano Sul Gizio, Italy,* Nat shared this story about growing up in Lewis Run, Pennsylvania:

> "I also remember my first ride on a Model "T" [Ford] from Lewis Run to Bradford with Ma and Mr. Monago,

who owned a store in Lewis Run. I also remember getting into mischief on Halloween tipping over "outhouses" and stealing fruit and vegetables from trucks that used to come to Lewis Run. We also used to sell junk to Mr. Lovitz, from Bradford, after we took it off his truck. We used to get 25 cents to 50 cents just to buy ice cream."

Little did Nat know that in only a few short years he would be fighting a war across Europe

- While riding in a 32-ton Sherman tank instead of a Model "T" Ford;
- Would be shooting at the enemy and blowing up buildings instead of tipping over "outhouses";
- Would be scavenging the French, Belgian, Dutch, and German countrysides for fruit, vegetables, eggs, and meat to supplement his Army rations;
- Would be making junk out of the German fighting equipment and not selling it; and
- Wouldn't see any ice cream until many months after landing in France (June 12, 1944, six days after D-Day).

This account now focuses on Nat's military service and experiences from his enlistment in the U.S. Army on February 10, 1942, until his honorable discharge on October 21, 1945 (3 years, 8 months, 11 days). It also includes a summary of his life after his discharge through his passing in 2012.

III. STATESIDE MILITARY SERVICE

"Never, never, never believe any war will be smooth and easy, or that anyone who embarks on the strange voyage can measure the tides and hurricanes he will encounter. The statesman who yields to war fever must realize that once the signal is given, he is no longer the master of policy but the slave of unforeseeable and uncontrollable events." (England's Prime Minister Winston Churchill, *Observation on War*)

In September 1940, the U.S. Congress passed the Selective Service and Training Act. This was the first peacetime draft in U.S. history for males ages 21 and older. The term of service for inductees was set for just one year. Then, in the summer of 1941, with the world situation continuing to deteriorate, Congress passed the Service Extension Act by a single vote. On Sunday, December 7, 1941, the Japanese bombed Pearl Harbor, Hawaii. Nat remembers hearing about it while listening to the news bulletins on the radio. (There was no television in those days.) Congress immediately declared war on the Axis (Germany, Italy, and Japan) the next day on Monday, December 8, 1941. Following the attack, Congress amended the draft law and extended the term of service from one year to the duration plus six months. Then, about a year later on November 13, 1942, Congress lowered the minimum draft age from 21 to 18 because the U.S. Armed Forces were now becoming engaged in combat and suffered many casualties. Draft registration was now compulsory for all males between the ages of 18 and 65, with only those between 20 and 45 eligible to be drafted.

The author's father, "Barb" Costanzo, (Nat's brother-in-law), who was 41 at the time and married and with a family of seven (7) children, was now subject to the draft. However, he was never called up because of his age and family situation which gave him a low classification of "4-A." However, anyone classified as "1-A" was immediately available to be drafted. It didn't take long to go from being a civilian to being in the Armed Forces once you were classified as "1-A." For example, the author was classified as "1-A" as soon as he reached his 18th birthday on April 15, 1945. He graduated from high school on June 10, 1945, took his pre-induction physical examination on June 23, 1945, and was inducted into the U.S. Army on July 23, 1945, along with three married men with families and in their mid-30's from Lewis Run (Mike "Friday" Ross, Louie

Pantuso, and Frank Benedict). Some members of the author's high school class, who reached 18 before he did in their senior year, were drafted before they could complete high school. They were needed as replacements for the many Americans who had been killed or wounded during the fighting in Europe and in the island-hopping campaigns in the Pacific.

Now every able-bodied U.S. male between the ages of 18 and 45 had to think about whether he should enlist right away or wait until he was drafted. Nat was aware that some of his friends had already been drafted or enlisted. His brother, Clemente (Clem), had already enlisted into the Army in January 1941 and was stationed at Camp Upton, NY. Nat was now 22 years old and was classified "1-A." However, he knew if he enlisted, he could choose his branch of service— the Army (which included the Army Air Corps), or Navy, or Marine Corps. He didn't want to be drafted, yet he wanted to serve his country, but only in the U.S. Army. So, he enlisted in the Army on February 10, 1942, at the age of 22, along with his friend, Matt Langianese, from Lewis Run. Matt was one of five brothers with military service in WWII. Their father, Mike Langianese, Sr., served with the U.S. Army in France in World War I (1917-1918).

In no time, Nat found himself on a train leaving the familiar Allegheny Mountains heading for his basic training at the Fort Knox, KY Armored Training Center. He was now part of the United States' large fighting army. It didn't take him long to realize that he had to make many readjustments to his previous habits and lifestyle. One month after enlisting, Nat wrote this in a letter to his 17-year-old nephew, Carl Costanzo, about his first 38 days in the Army:

> "...Don't worry about my feet, kid. I've got a 10 ½ EE shoe and I got plenty of room to spare. We do a lot of riding anyway. Yesterday we went on a motor hike in a big Scout Car for 30 miles. Some fun...I have to shine three pairs of shoes, shave, take a shower, and straighten out my footlocker for inspection tomorrow. /s/ Your Uncle Sam, Naz"

Nat's brother-in-law, "Barb" Costanzo, owned and operated a barbershop in Lewis Run. Many of his customers had now left Lewis Run to serve in the military. They knew that he had been collecting their postcards and displaying them on the large mirrors in his barbershop. So, on February 26, 1942, some two weeks after Nat enlisted, he sent this card to "Barb:"

> "Hi Barb: I told you I would send you a picture of the motorized units here [Fort Knox, KY], so here it is. I've written three letters already tonite. Last nite I wrote 17 cards. The sun was out today, but the air was cold. I hear Steve Chohrach* was home last week. That's fine.

I don't expect to be home for about 4 weeks. That's if we don't go west. Nat" *(Underline added.)*

(*Note: Steve Chochrach was one of the first men from Lewis Run to enlist in the Army Air Corps. He joined in 1939 and became a radioman and gunner on a B-25 bomber patrolling the East Coast of the United States looking for German submarines. Shortly after he was home on leave, Steve was reported missing in action on March 5, 1942, and was later declared dead when his bomber was lost over the Atlantic Ocean. He was 22 years old. The story of his crew was featured in the March 22, 1942 article in the *New York Herald Tribune* and in the August 23, 1942 "Picture Parade Magazine" section of the *Philadelphia Inquirer*.)

Because Nat demonstrated outstanding leadership qualities to his instructors during his basic training, he was selected to remain at Fort Knox to train other soldiers scheduled for armored units. He was assigned to the Armored Force School Demonstration Regiment. His training for new groups of recruits was conducted in 16-week increments. It included, among many things, 25-mile foot and motor marches, crawling under barbed wire with live machine gun bullets fired over the trainees' heads, and tank warfare gunnery and tactics. Nat remembered that it was a very grueling time for him—the hours were long and his training schedule very demanding. Most of his new draftees were from New York and New Jersey.

They didn't know their left foot from their right one when it came to know how to march. So, he had them hold a broom handle in their left hand until they learned how to march.

Nat also traveled around the country taking men from Fort Knox to other Army posts on the East Coast and the West Coast. While a Private, he took some soldiers to Fort Bragg, NC. He sent this postcard to "Barb" on May 20, 1942:

> "Hi Barb: <u>Here's a good one for your mirror.</u> Are you surprised to hear from me? Boy, I'm certainly seeing the country. As you know, I took some men to Ft. Bragg. We arrived at midnite Tues. We'll be in Knox on Thurs. Boy, the <u>southern gals are O.K. down here.</u> Write when you have time. Naz" *(Underlines added.)*

Then on August 21, 1942, he sent this postcard to "Barb" from Los Angeles, CA, after he was recently promoted to Lance Corporal. He oversaw a railroad passenger carload of soldiers on a troop train traveling from Fort Knox, KY to Indio, CA. The cross-country train trip took a week.

> "Hi Barb: Just a card from the Southwest. *[Map showing Arizona's National Monuments]* Had a nice trip. I'm now in Angeles having a peach of a time. Tell the gang hello. <u>Here's another for the mirror.</u> Naz" *(Underline added.)*

He returned to Fort Knox, KY on August 28, 1942, and wrote this on another postcard to "Barb:"

"Hi Barb: I am back in camp, but I still have some cards from Calif. so I am sending one. *[Photograph of the Earl Carroll Theatre in Hollywood, California with a sign 'Seats Reserved in Advance—$2.50']* Boy is this some theatre. I was in it Sun[day]. You ought to see the fixtures, dance floor, tables, and whatnot. Hello to all. Best of luck. Naz"

While in Los Angeles, he went to hear the Freddie Martin Dance Orchestra at the Earl Carroll Theater. It was one of the famous dance bands of that era. He was also in the audience for a radio show like "The Price is Right" show on TV today. He didn't remember if anyone in Lewis Run knew he was on the radio.

Nat's brother, Clem, was now a Sergeant and stationed in Australia in the Administrative Section of the 2nd Replacement Depot. On October 29, 1942, Clem wrote in a letter to his brother, Jim, nicknamed "Slug," that:

"Naz was telling me about our pictures being in Woolworth's window *[a department store in Bradford, PA]*. It certainly was a great idea of someone's, I guess Mom was pretty happy about the whole thing. Did you happen to take a picture of it? I would like to see the display if possible. Any chance???"

While at Fort Knox, Nat met a "southern gal," Frances (Fran) Burgy, from Louisville, KY. Nat lived in a room on the first floor of his barracks at Fort Knox. His Mess Sergeant, Benny Roddy, lived in a room upstairs above him. Benny was married, and he and his wife were invited to Thanksgiving dinner in November 1942 in Louisville with friends. Benny asked Nat to join them and promised him that he would meet "a nice girl, who was bowlegged, had pearly teeth and had straight hair." They all attended church and then went to dinner. Nat said it was "love at first sight." The romance blossomed when Frances bought tickets for them to attend the 1943 New Year's Eve dance at the Grand Hotel in Louisville. They danced until five in the morning as they drank rum and cokes. Since Frances' mother was a policewoman at the Brown-Forman Distillers in Louisville, they had no trouble getting the "booze," which was hard to get. The romance moved forward rapidly. Eventually, news of it came to Lewis Run.

About once a week, Nat's oldest sister, Fannie, wrote letters to her three brothers in the service—Frank, Nat, and Clem—for her parents who could read and write in Italian, but not in English. She would also read to her mother any letters written by her brothers. This one day, Fannie and her mother were having coffee with a neighbor who was also the mother of Nat's Lewis Run girlfriend. Fannie opened and read one of Nat's letters. They were shocked to hear that he had met a beautiful girl in Louisville "who could sew," and he was going to marry her. They all cried after hearing the news.

On July 21, 1943, Nat sent this postcard to his sister, Vincie, and her husband, "Barb," from Fort Knox, KY:

> "Hello you all, I guess it's about time I wrote you and Vincie a card. I've been very busy. Here's hoping you will be able to make the wedding August 21st. Tell all the kids hello. Weather is hot. War news now on the air. Nice club we have on front of card [Non-commissioned Officers Club, Fort Knox, KY]. Love, Naz" (Underlines added.)

Nat and Fran were married on August 21, 1943, nine months after they met. The wedding was held in the Catholic Church across the street from Fran's home.

Fannie, her father, and two sisters, Virginia and Vera, left Bradford to travel to Louisville for the wedding. They rode on the Baltimore and Ohio Railroad for Pittsburgh, PA where they had to change trains for Louisville. The trains were crowded with servicemen. So, for most of the trip, the Piscitelli's had to sit on their suitcases in the aisles or stand up hanging on the bars over the windows. Since they had never met Fran, it was arranged that Nat's family would recognize her by her blue cape and a hat. She was told to look for a gentleman with a mustache traveling with three women. After easily recognizing each other at the train station, they went to Fran's house where they met her mother, Mrs. Frances Burgy, and had dinner.

While in Kentucky, Nat arranged for his family to take a tour of Fort Knox in an Army vehicle. After the tour, they had a family "sit down" dinner of roast beef served on a white sheet for a tablecloth at a mess hall on Fort Knox. The meal was prepared by Nat's Mess Sergeant, Benny, who was also one of the ushers at the wedding. Fannie, who is a great cook, enjoyed the dinner. She was very impressed by the Army's large walk-in refrigerator because she, like many others in Lewis Run, only had a small icebox most of her life.

Nat's sister, Virginia, will always remember her trip to Louisville. She stayed at the home of Fran's friends, Paul and Millie Allsmiller. While washing her hands, Virginia lost her engagement ring when it fell down the sink's drain. On arriving home, her husband, Mike Sylvester, told her to go to Clayton's Jewelry Store in Bradford and buy another one. Virginia's daughter, Phyllis, now has her mother's ring.

The Piscitelli's stayed a week in Louisville and returned to Lewis Run after the wedding. They were followed soon thereafter by Nat and Fran. She put on her wedding gown for Nat's family. They had another wedding reception in Lewis Run for those relatives who could not attend the Louisville ceremony. Fannie remembered that Nat's ex-girlfriend and her mother, who lived next door, still were shocked by the news and were seen crying as the family celebrated.

Nat and Fran celebrated their 64th wedding anniversary in 2007. Fran passed away on January 27, 2008, at the age of 89. Nat passed away on February 27, 2012, at the age of 92.

IV. OVERSEAS MILITARY SERVICE

(WESTERN EUROPE)
(MAY 21, 1944 TO SEPTEMBER 30, 1945)

TRIP OVERSEAS (NEW YORK TO ENGLAND)
(MAY 21-30, 1944)

Nat, who was now a Sergeant, was notified in early 1944 that he was being assigned overseas to England as an individual replacement rather than being shipped out with a unit. He was shocked but was willing to go even though his wife, Frances, was expecting their first child. She kept busy at home making the baby's layette. Her visiting nurse was so impressed with the baby's clothes that she wanted to display them at one of the Louisville stores. Frances said no because she didn't want to get the layette soiled. Since a sonogram wasn't available then to verify the sex of the baby, Frances likes to say today that, if her first baby was a boy, he would have had "lace on his panties." She stayed with her mother in Louisville, KY while Nat was overseas.

Their daughter, Margaret (Peggy) Anne, was born on May 20, 1944, one day before Nat sailed from New York for England. He didn't find out about her birth until some eight weeks later when he received a letter from his sister, Vera. His standing joke is: "I'm still waiting to be notified by the Red Cross." Shortly after the baby was born, Nat's mother and Vera went by train to Louisville to see Fran and Peggy Anne. Here is what Vera wrote on a postcard to the Costanzo Family on June 5, 1944:

"Hello Everybody, Am just fine & having a swell rest. Weather is pretty hot down here tho. Fran & baby are doing nicely. See you soon. Take care of yourselves. Love, Mom & Vera"

Nat departed from Camp Shanks, NY on May 21, 1944, aboard a converted Liberty troopship transport bound for England. The ship was part of a convoy that zig-zagged its way over 3,600 miles across the Atlantic Ocean to avoid the many German submarines (U-boats). He commented that the food was lousy, especially the greasy pork chops, which he "upchucked."

Nat slept on deck most of the time because the ship's quarters were too crowded. He passed the time away by playing cards and worrying about what would happen to him after he landed in England.

Author, Belten Y. Cooper, describes the conditions on the transport in this manner:

> "...the enlisted men slept in the holds in bunks stacked five high. Each of the men had a space approximately two feet by two feet by six feet for himself and his duffel bag. The bag, about eighteen inches in diameter and thirty-six inches long, held all of the soldier's personal gear. Obviously, the soldier was crowded in his bunk. Under the double loading arrangement, soldiers spent twelve hours in their bunks and the next twelve hours on deck. They would bring their duffle bags with them wherever they went, because they may not return to their same bunk."

The crossing to Liverpool, England took 10 days. Nat landed there on May 30, 1944.

ADVANCED ARMORED TRAINING IN ENGLAND (MAY 31-JUNE 11, 1944)

After his landing in England, Nat underwent advanced training in tank warfare. It was conducted by U.S. veterans of the 1st Armored Division, who had fought and survived the 1943 fighting in North Africa against the German Africa Korps of General Erwin Rommel ("The Desert Fox"). The war in Africa was the American Army's first taste of fighting the Germans. Nat's training was conducted in the English countryside and consisted of tank maneuvers and deployment tactics learned from the armored battles in North Africa.

While in England, Nat met Johnny Pingie, a friend from his hometown of Lewis Run, PA, who later, like Nat, was assigned to the 2nd Armored Division. He also met Charlie Di Fonzo, a friend from Buffalo, New York.

Upon completion of about 10 days of training, Nat again boarded a ship at Liverpool, England on June 11, 1944 (5 days after the D-Day landings on June 6, 1944, on the coast of France). He landed at Omaha Beach, France on June 12, 1944. He had crossed the English Channel in less than 24 hours. He recalls the beach was a mess with dead men, vehicles and other equipment and scattered supplies.

ASSIGNMENT TO 2ND ARMORED DIVISION IN NORMANDY, FRANCE (JUNE 12, 1944)

From Omaha Beach, he went by truck to "God knows where" with shells falling all around the vehicle. This was his first experience of being under enemy fire, and he was scared.

He arrived in a replacement depot ("Repple Depple") with several replacements—privates, sergeants, and lieutenants. They were received by a First Sergeant who greeted them with "You had better give your hearts to God because I got your 'ass.' Now get off the truck!" This was a reception that he will never forget.

From there, he was assigned as an individual replacement to Company E, 2nd Battalion, 66th Armored Regiment, 2nd Armored Division ("Hell on Wheels"). The unit was the first armored division to land in France during D-Day. He was now one of the 10,341 enlisted men assigned to the division. There, Nat was now part of a five-man crew and was assigned as the driver of a 32-ton M4 Sherman medium tank with a 75mm gun and other armaments.

> "The M4 Sherman normally had a <u>five-man crew</u>: the <u>driver</u>; the <u>assistant driver</u>, who rode next to him and manned the ball-mount 30-caliber machine gun which was particularly effective against infantry; the <u>assistant gunner</u>, who sat on the left side of the turret and loaded the main gun; the <u>gunner</u>, who sat on the right side of the turret and fired the gun; and the <u>tank commander</u>, who sat at the rear of the turret and operated the radio. There was a small cupola with the periscopic sight in the hatch cover directly over the tank commander. When the tank was under artillery fire, the tank commander kept the hatch closed and buttoned up; however, the tank commander often rode with the hatch open for better visibility." (Cooper, p. 192) *(Underlines added.)*

The tank commander was also responsible for operating a .50-caliber machine gun mounted on the turret. It was movable in all directions, including upward to provide anti-aircraft protection. However, there was one big drawback to the gun's location on the tank. The tank commander had to climb out of the turret to operate it. This made him very vulnerable to enemy shell fire. But, as the war progressed and as the Allies achieved air superiority, the .50-caliber machine guns were removed from the tanks in Nat's unit and given to the infantry soldiers for added firepower. It was found to be an excellent weapon against ground troops. It was the "envy of the German Army and the pride of the G.I." (Irwin, pp. 32, 114)

The gunner had a .30-caliber coaxially mounted machine gun alongside his 75mm cannon, later modified to 76mm. The two weapons moved together on the same axis and were both zeroed in to hit the target at 1,800 yards. The gunner would normally fire a tracer round from his machine gun to find the range to a target and then fire his cannon to score a hit. (Irwin, p. 32)

Nat's first reaction when joining his unit was one of being scared. The veterans in his unit, who had already been in action earlier with the 2nd Armored Division in North Africa and Sicily, received him as "just another soldier." They were glad to have the replacements, even though they were "green and scared." All soldiers, whether they want to admit it or not, are scared when they enter combat for the first time. Nat was no exception.

Stephen Ambrose, the noted historian, described "combat" this way:

> "Combat requires all the nerves, all the physical attributes, every bit of training. It is only in combat, nowhere else, where time is measured in other ways than by clocks or calendars. Only in combat does the soldier realize that he is in the worst situation than can ever be imagined, that nothing else can compare to it, that the longer he stays where he is the more likely that he will be dead, or if he is extremely lucky he will be wounded. Only in combat is one in position in which youngsters his age he doesn't know, has never met, are trying to kill him—and he is trying to kill them." (Ambrose, *Comrades*, p. 109)

Nat's first tank was named "El Celeste" after his Tank Commander's wife. It was home for its crew members for many days at a time. Their cross training was critical. Each crew member had to learn each other's job and how to live with and to rely on each other. Nat found out very quickly that his life was not going to be a "...daily regime of personal activities such as eating, drinking, hygiene, recreation,

or sleeping..." (Irwin, p. 34). He was going to have to learn
to do these things whenever the opportunity presented itself.

Nat's tank battalion's table of organization for men and
equipment called for 40-officers, 689-enlisted men, 77-M4
Sherman tanks, and 86-other vehicles. The division had a total
of 657-officers, 10,341-enlisted men, 269-M4 Sherman tanks,
1,141-other vehicles, 54-105mm howitzers, 9-75mm howitzers, and 30-57mm anti-tank guns. It was one of only two
oversized, powerful, "heavy" armored divisions in the U.S.
Army. They were created and conceived by General Patton
to raise havoc on the enemy through its mobility, firepower,
and shock action. (Cooper, pp. 48, 61)

Nat's type of division did not move "on its stomach but on
gasoline." It required eight times the tonnage in gasoline for
its vehicles than it needed in food to feed the troops. (General
Omar Bradley, *Soldier's Story*, pp. 245, 565)

> "A full combat load (3-day supply) for our division alone
> was more than 300,000 gallons (of gasoline), which
> amounted to three hundred GMC 2 1/2-ton trucks each
> carrying 1,000 gallons in (200) 5-gallon cans." Each
> tank had a range of 80 miles under average conditions
> with its full fuel capacity of 200 gallons (40 5-gallon
> cans) of gasoline. Germans would continue to shoot
> their lethal 88mm guns at a stopped tank's fuel supply

until the tank caught fire. It would become a "flaming death trap" for the crew as the gasoline, ammo, and other parts of the tank burned. U.S. troops called the tank a 'Ronson', after an American made cigarette lighter advertised as "always lighting up the first time." (Cooper, pp. 89, 127, 314)

But it was not named after the famous "Zippo" lighter made in Bradford, PA (6 miles from Nat's hometown) and carried by many service personnel in WWII.

Two of Nat's tanks caught fire from hits by German shells. When this happened, he and the crew jumped out of their tank and "ran like Hell!" He also saw many US tanks go up in flames, killing or wounding many of their crews. It was not a pleasant sight and one that he vividly remembers to this day. David Holbrook describes it this way:

"Tanks burn in a way that has its own grotesque poignancy. The flames are explosively fierce and yet are tightly contained in the hollow steel shell; so, the smoke rushed out with tumbling fury. From the turret, black smoke alternating with intense flames thunders forth in a monstrous jet. But then from time to time, the flame is forced into huge expelled puffs by the exploding shells within. Each black puff from the circular turret hatch becomes with grotesque perfection a rolling smoke ring. Such smoke ring we associate with quiet reflective moments—old men showing their skill with a pipe in the chimney-corner, to admiring children. The perfect black smoke ring shooting up from a burning tank suggested some grotesque devil's game in the thing, a derisory joke of the fiends, over dying men. A burning tank, because of this, looked like a monster, a dying dragon, vomiting up life within its black guts, and blowing aloft ghostly rings, which mounted, curling in on themselves, high into the air. Beneath these sad signals, a red and white glower would roll in the eyes of the dead monster, the hatch holes, through which the crew had entered never to emerge again." (David Holbrook, *Flesh Wounds*, p. 131)

EXPANDING AND BREAKING OUT FROM THE NORMANDY BEACHHEAD AND HEDGEROW FIGHTING (JUNE 13-JULY 25, 1944)

Nat's first combat action took place in the middle of June 1944 around the town of Carentan, France, 10 miles inland from Omaha Beach. His unit's mission was to break through the enemy lines and move inland to reinforce the 101st Airborne Division, whose paratroopers and equipment were parachuted in and were also landed in gliders in the pre-dawn darkness on D-Day, June 6, 1944.

The fighting was very intense because the Germans were using the French "hedgerows" (mounds of root-packed earth 6-8 feet high, 10-12 feet wide at the base, and overgrown with trees and tangled with vines and brush to divide French properties). These hedgerows were a maze created by their many ditches and sunken roads. They acted as natural concealment and cover for the German troops waiting in ambush with their machine guns, artillery, tanks, anti-tank mines, and anti-tank guns (panzerfausts—"tank fists"). The existence of these hedgerows, which extended 10-40 miles inland from Omaha Beach, were not reported by Army Intelligence as obstacles to alert U.S. troops as to their locations and formidability. The Germans clobbered the Americans there. Consequently, they became "death traps" for the American Army's "green" troops and cost them dearly in lives and equipment as they fought to survive their first battles. (Cooper, pp. 8-10) (Gerard, pp. 149, 150, 153)

> "An 88mm shell has a high muzzle velocity—that means it shoots in faster than the speed of sound on a flat trajectory...with a noise like a freight train. It is not very big, about the circumference of a cocktail shaker, but longer and heavier, weighing 22 pounds, with a sharply-pointed nose." (Gerard, pp. 184, 282)

> "...when such round (armor-piercing shot) hit (a tank) solidly home, the effects were instantaneously horrible.

At least, if the shot lodged but did not penetrate, the blow to the face of the armour [sic] detached high-speed fragments from the rear into the (tank's) interior, which inflicted multiple small wounds on the crew. If the shot penetrated, it would retain some of its velocity but be confined by the armoured [sic] skin and so ricochet about inside, smashing all it touched, metal or flesh. At worst, it would ignite ammunition and fuel—which first was immaterial, since they burnt together—incinerating whoever could not reach the hatch." (John Keegan, *Six Armies in Normandy from D-Day to the Liberation of Paris*, p. 198)

These hedgerows could only be penetrated by a tank with a bulldozer blade attached to it. It took an American sergeant, with experience as a farm boy clearing farmland, to come up with an idea for a new device to penetrate hedgerows. He fastened to the front of a tank a steel base channel with about a dozen 10-12 inch long, pointed, triangular-shaped spikes welded perpendicular to the base channel. Because the spikes looked like the horns of a rhinoceros, it was called a "Rhino" tank. It was designed as a plow to cut through and level the hedgerows. They were installed on many tanks with the steel for the cutting blades coming from the German obstacles installed on the Normandy beaches. This feature of the "hedge chopper" gave our soldiers some satisfaction. However, there were only four of these tanks in Nat's entire division, and his tank was not one of them. (Cooper, page 45; General Eisenhower, page 269)

In this battle around Carentan, Nat's company (about 150-200 men), as a unit in the 66th Armored Regiment of the 2nd Armored Division, assisted in defeating the German 6th Parachute Regiment and the 37th SS Panzer Regiment. It was after this action that the 2nd Armored Division earned the nickname of "Roosevelt's Butchers." (Donald E. Houston, *Hell on Wheels, The 2nd Armored Division*, p. 204)

During the rest of June and in early July 1944, Nat's unit was primarily in a reserve role. They learned how to camouflage their tanks and their clothing, how to perform needed maintenance on their tanks and weapons, how to integrate tank-infantry-artillery forces and weapons in hedgerow fighting, and how the Germans used their tanks and anti-tank weapons. (Houston, p. 205)

During July 18-24, 1944, Nat's unit was again in reserve after turning over its part of the front line to the British forces. Time was spent attending demonstrations of tank-infantry teamwork in hedgerow country by infantry troops learning how to ride tanks and how tanks can help support them with the tank's weapons. A new device, an external telephone, was now mounted on a tank so an infantryman working alongside it could talk to the tank commander. Each tank was now to carry three days of food rations for its crew and supporting infantry. In addition, each tank now carried extra ammo and gasoline for 200 miles of operation. Also, each tank carried extra shovels, picks, and axes (pioneer tools) so its accompanying infantry could dig their foxholes and slit trenches faster and, more importantly, to create a feeling that tankers wanted and needed them. (Houston, p. 208)

Occasionally during this time, Nat's unit practiced this tank-infantry-artillery teamwork with limited objective attacks in the hedgerows to expand the Normandy Beachhead by securing key terrain features and roads and to capture prisoners. The Germans put up strong resistance as the US forces attempted to move forward; consequently, no real breakthrough was achieved. However, the "green" American troops were learning how to fight the hard way—on the job with the Germans doing the instructing. (General Robert H. Scales, *Certain Victory: The US Army in the Gulf War*, pp. 6, 11)

General Eisenhower summarized these operations as follows:

"The Battle of the Beachhead was a period of incessant and heavy fighting and one, which except for the capture of Cherbourg, showed few geographical gains. Yet it was during this period that the stage was set for the later, spectacular liberation of France and Belgium. The struggle in the beachhead was responsible for many developments, both material and doctrinal, that stood in good stead throughout the remainder of the war. It was dogged 'doughboy' fighting at its worst. Every division that participated in it came out of action hardened, battle-wise, and self-confident." (General Eisenhower, pp. 256, 257, 269)

The final breakout from the Omaha Beachhead was initiated on July 25, 1944, by Operation COBRA when 2,430 Allied aircraft dropped 4,000 tons of bombs and napalm (a jellied inflammable mixture which explodes on impact into a hot ball of fire) in the vicinity of St. Lo, France to smash the hedgerows and German troops.

Nat was aware that, in one terrible "Friendly Fire" incident that day, our own bombs were dropped on many of our troops, killing 111 GIs and wounding 490.

Also, a former resident of Lewis Run, Private First-Class John De Fillippo, 21 years old, was killed on the day of the bombing.

Nat identified his tank with a colored identification panel over its rear deck so that it could be seen by friendly aircraft. However, on July 26, 1944, his unit was one of several attacked by a flight of American P-47 "Thunderbolt" fighter bombers. The bombers mistook them for Germans even though the

Americans were using their identification panels and yellow smoke to signal the planes. (Houston, p. 216)

Nat's tank was not hit; however, a tank manned by his Company Commander was destroyed. The Company Commander and the rest of the tank crew were killed as a result of this "Friendly Fire" incident.

It was at St. Lo that Nat was promoted to Staff Sergeant and designated a Tank Commander.

BREAKOUT AND THE RACE ACROSS FRANCE, BELGIUM, HOLLAND, AND INTO GERMANY (JULY 26-SEPTEMBER 18, 1944)

General Patton spoke of this phase of the war as "The crust is broken, now it's time to eat the pie." ("Patton," *A&E Channel*, June 8, 2003)

After the breakout from the hedgerow country, Nat's unit moved 30 to 40 miles a day with little opposition from the German forces.

> "An Armored column on the move is one of the most awesome sights I ever hope to see—those big, rumbling monster-looking tanks, tank destroyers, half-tracks, etc. A tank always makes me think of some prehistoric animal—like a dinosaur or something.

Then all that grinding, growling noise. You feel like
they're eager to fight & that nothing can stop them.
But the Krauts (the Germans) may have just as many,
& of course, a tank can be stopped. Just the same they
look formidable & fearsome & you're glad we have so
many." (Janice Holt Giles, *The G.I Journal of Sergeant
Giles,* p. 63)

Most of the time, Nat's company was leading the advance. On
August 19, 1944, they attacked to cut off the German forces
from the Seine River between Elbeuf to the north and Paris
to the south, known as the Argentan-Falaise Pocket. It was
near Elbeuf that his tank was knocked out by German artillery fire. None of his crew were killed or wounded. His tank
was evacuated to the rear for repairs. He was issued another
tank. He had no way of knowing if anyone in that tank had
been previously killed or wounded before it was repaired and
placed back into action.

Members of Nat's 2nd Battalion received the Distinguished
Unit Citation for their outstanding performance during the
period July 26 to August 12, 1944, as they supported the
advance of the 2nd Armored Division. This award is only
given to select units and is prized by those who earn it.

Nat's unit raced across France pursuing the retreating
German Army.

Nat crossed from France into Belgium on September 2, 1944, and into Holland on September 11, 1944. They were moving so fast that they didn't even see the names of the towns they were liberating. Rumors were "flying around" now that the war in Europe would be over by Christmas. "Rumors, next to mail and food, are the lifeblood of military existence." (Irwin, p. 5) He began to have thoughts about being home for Christmas to see his wife and new daughter and to celebrate his 25th birthday. He felt good about this rate of advancement, but they began to run out of gasoline as they overextended their supply lines. This was a "double whammy" because his crew also needed gasoline to wash out their greasy tank uniforms!

His unit initially entered Germany on September 18, 1944, near Aachen, the ancient birthplace and citadel of King Charlemagne, and the seat of the Holy Roman Empire. Hitler ordered his armies "to hold Aachen at all costs." The battle of Belgium was now over (for a while anyway), and the battle for Germany had begun.

While Nat's unit was in Belgium, he was issued the new M4A1 Sherman tank with a more powerful 76mm gun. He was now better equipped to knock out German tanks with this more powerful gun. However, the Sherman tank was still outgunned by the German Tiger tank with its 88mm gun and its much thicker armor.

NAT'S "TYPICAL DAY" WHILE IN CONTACT WITH THE ENEMY

His "typical" day when his unit was advancing was to move in a column formation and to stay in contact over the tank's intercom with his crew telling them what to do and also by radio with the other tank commanders in his unit to get their battle orders. When they halted or at nightfall, his unit would circle their tanks off the road and establish a perimeter defense with their tanks and accompanying infantry so that the maintenance, supply, and medics could get their work done in preparation for the next day's action. Generally, his crew would service their tank, replenish their fuel and ammo, wash their clothes, and eat "K" rations. When they came under German air attack, they would try to drive their tank undercover and camouflage it. This didn't happen very often because the Allies had established air superiority. If any German plane got through the Allies' air space, it was called "Bed Check Charlie" by the U.S. troops because the plane seemed to come around just about "bedtime."

ASSAULT ON GERMANY AND THE SIEGFRIED LINE (SEPTEMBER 18 TO DECEMBER 19, 1944)

Once his unit was in Germany, it was now faced with fighting the enemy entrenched in the Siegfried Line and in the city of Aachen. The Siegfried Line, sometimes called the "West Wall," was constructed by Hitler in the late 1930s in response to France's fortification, the Maginot Line, built along its eastern border with Germany.

The Siegfried Line was an effective defensive system consisting of an intricate series of concrete dragons' teeth, 20,000 concrete pillboxes, interconnected communication trenches, gun pits, minefields, fortified villages, and foxholes supported by an excellent road net. Its fortifications varied in depth from 10 to 40 miles and extended for 940 miles along the German border from near Basel, Switzerland to Kleve in northern Germany. (Cooper, pp. 122-124)

The terrain and obstacles were far different from what Nat had seen in France and Belgium. The German forces used their land features and Siegfried Line fortifications to put up stiffer resistance, and the 2nd Armored Division fought through this heavy combat suffering heavy tank losses, particularly around the German city of Aachen.

The rainy, miserable weather in October and November 1944 didn't help much either. The division's tanks had difficulty negotiating the soft ground and muddy terrain. The 2nd Armored Division lost approximately 100 tanks before the unit reached the Roer River on November 28, 1944. They assumed defensive positions there until it was released as a result of the German Ardennes Counteroffensive ("Battle of the Bulge"), initiated on December 16, 1944. (Cooper, p. 155)

Nat had his second tank knocked out around Aachen. A German artillery shell hit the engine while his tank was in a position on the front line. Fortunately, his crew suffered no casualties. He was again pulled out of the frontline for three days while the engine was replaced.

He had now been in almost daily contact with the enemy for the past six months. After his tank was knocked out the second time, he was feeling the "war was catching up with him," already had "two strikes against him" and, with the "third strike," he could be "out." On December 11, 1944, he wrote this to his Mom and Dad:

> "Tonet (Nat's sister) said you were worried about me. Maybe I made a mistake when I wrote and said my nerves were bad. Am at a rest area now and getting plenty of sleep and plenty to eat."

On December 13, 1944, while still in Germany, he wrote, in what he called "a dehydrated letter," the name he gave to V-Mail, to his Mom and Dad to let them know that he was fine.

Nat was aware that one of his Lewis Run, PA friends, Johnny Monago, was captured in North Africa in 1942 and was in a German Prisoner of War (POW) camp. In Nat's letter of December 13, 1944, he wrote:

"I don't know if I'm allowed to write to Johnny Monago or not, I'll find out, but in the meantime send me his address. I think I am about 25 miles from him. We'll do our damnest [sic] to get him out."

Nat also wrote in his December 13, 1944 letter that he was making plans to visit during Christmas with Matt Langianese, his friend from Lewis Run, PA, who enlisted with Nat and was in a nearby signal unit. He was also planning to meet with Johnny Pingie, another friend from Lewis Run who was also in the 2nd Armored Division. Nat wrote:

"...the weather as usual is snowy...It would be nice if we (Matt and Johnny) could spend Xmas together even if we have to stop once in a while to shoot up a few Krauts (Germans)."

This meeting with Johnny Pingie happened two days later on December 15, 1944, when Nat wrote to his Mom and Dad that:

"I saw Johnny Pingie ride by in a tank today and he hollered back that he would see me soon. I only hope that we three (Nat, Matt, and Johnny) can get together for Xmas. God permitting we will. Just had a nice hot cup of coffee and some swell fruitcake. You sure do have a lot of snow. I hope I was back shoveling it too."

NAT'S PARTICIPATION IN THE
"BATTLE OF THE BULGE"
(DECEMBER 20, 1944 TO JANUARY 4, 1945)

In the snowy dawn of December 16, 1944, the Germans launched a massive assault westward toward Belgium through the American forces in the Luxembourg-Ardennes—a heavily forested area, and south of Nat's unit. The German code word for the attack was "Greif," in English, "Grab," which the Americans soon translated to "grief." This is known as the "Battle of the Bulge" and was the German's attempt to put a bulge in the Allies line and grab the strategic port of Antwerp, Belgium.

The initial assault against the U.S. Army's green front-line troops was overwhelming, and they were pushed back. Nat's 2nd Armored Division was ordered to pull back some 70-75 miles from their positions in Germany on the west side of the Roer River and return as quickly as possible to Belgium. This was accomplished on December 20-22, 1944 to help brunt the German thrust. It was one of the most spectacular moves of the war over roads covered with ice, snow, and mud and invisibility hampered by fog.

In Nat's letter of December 20, 1944, to his Mom and Dad, he was still in Germany and was preparing to move out. He had received their "swell" package, mailed on October 9, 1944 (2-1/2 months ago). He wrote:

"The meatballs were delicious. The socks are just the thing. The cookies and other foodstuffs are swell. I am getting the tank stocked-up so it looks like a grocery store.

"We had spaghetti for chow tonite and, I'm glad I saved the meatballs. I heated them and boy oh boy, they went swell with the spags. The boys in my crew really enjoyed them."

He then went on to say:

"I imagine you read the big push the Nazi's have started. Maybe it will wake up some of the people in the States to the fact that this war isn't quite over. Five more days until Xmas. Oh well, I'll try to enjoy myself. A Merry Xmas to all. Say hello to the friends.

Love Always,
Son, Nat"

When Nat's division traveled at night, its units traveled very slowly at the rate of six miles per hour under blackout conditions and with radio silence. They used "…only blackout lights—slits of light in a metal hood—it was hard to see anything…" while maintaining just enough distance between vehicles to see their blackout taillights called "cat's eyes"—two slivers of red. If the taillights merged into one, the vehicle ahead was too close. (Gerard, pp. 148, 278) Night vision goggles had not yet been invented.

During the daylight hours, the rate was doubled to 12 miles per hour and the interval increased to 75 yards. At regulation 50-yard intervals, the division's 3,000 vehicles would have formed a convoy over 100 miles long.

It was one of the most spectacular moves of the war over roads covered with ice, snow, mud and with visibility hampered by fog. Only 30 vehicles, out of nearly 3,000 in the 2nd Armored Division, failed to reach the assembly area in Belgium by midnight of December 22nd. (Steven Smith, *2nd Armored Division, "Hell on Wheels,"* p. 52)

Nat considered this "advance to the rear" as just another mission he must accomplish to the best of his crew's ability even though his division had fought long and hard the past two months to gain some ground in Germany.

The German surprise attack had split the American forces in the south from those in the north. The bulk of the Allied forces north of the Bulge were under the command of British General Montgomery. Even though Generals Eisenhower and Bradley had always resisted putting large units of American troops under British command, the 2nd Armored Division, along with other units in the U.S. Ninth Army, was placed under the control of the British General Montgomery's 21st Army Group in the north. At the time, this assignment made sense. (Houston, pp. 333, 334)

> "Later when the Bulge was all but over Montgomery would use the change of command, in a press conference on January 7, to claim for himself and the British armies the entire credit for saving the Allies and winning the victory. In fact, only a few British troops were used at all in the entire battle. This pompous claim would cause Bradley, usually the calmest and most considerate of men to threaten resignation if he had to serve under Montgomery, and Patton added that if Bradley went, so would he." (James Jones, *WWII*, p. 206)

During these initial days of the battle, the weather was very bad. The weather was cold with snow on the ground, a ground fog, and snow-laden clouds. In fact, it was Europe's coldest winter in the past 40 years with wind chills up to a minus 50 degrees below zero. Our troops were initially denied air support because of the bad weather. The Germans timed their offensive with that in mind. The scattered snow turned to freezing rain, making the roads a sheet of ice and very hazardous. Finally, on December 23-24, 1944, the weather cleared, and air support and aerial supplies began to be given to the beleaguered U.S. troops.

> "Two thousand Allied bombers screened by eight hundred fighters pounded crowded German roads in daylight, yielding high claims in enemy tanks and transports." (David Eisenhower, *Eisenhower At War 1943-1945*, p. 587)

On December 25, 1944 (Christmas Day), Nat celebrated his 25th birthday. The war didn't stop for either Christmas or his birthday! He spent the day in the vicinity of Celles, Belgium. The 2nd Armored Division was on the northern flank of the Bulge and in position to stop the German deep penetration into Belgium. He spent his birthday in his tank eating cold turkey sandwiches and drinking coffee and fighting Germans. His tank crew was trying to stay warm in the snow and cold as they carried out their assigned missions.

On December 26, 1944, the 2nd Armored Division was ordered to "...assault von Rundstedt's leading westbound panzer (tank) elements. In one of the most brilliantly conducted operations of the war, Harmon (MG Ernie Harmon, Commander, 2nd Armored Division, nicknamed "Old Gravel Voice") utterly destroyed the 2nd Panzer Division and ground the German attack to a final, humiliating halt." (General Bradley, p. 371)

The 2nd Armored Division caught the 2nd SS Panzer Division on the road at Celles and virtually annihilated it. (Cooper, p. 185) Nat's crew was happy with the outcome.

> "Had the 2nd Armored Division failed, the Germans would most probably have realized their goal of splitting the Allies and may have been able to achieve a stalemate on the western front." (Houston, p. 327)

On December 28, 1944, the 2nd Armored was relieved by the 83rd Infantry Division and moved to the vicinity of Rochefort, Belgium in the same bivouac area they had left a week earlier. The men were given a few days to refit, to conduct maintenance, to rest, and to open Christmas packages. They were also treated to two turkey dinners—one for which they missed at Christmas and one for the upcoming New Year. (Houston, pages 350 and 353) During this time, Nat was not aware that the Germans had executed 81 American prisoners at Malmedy, Belgium during the Battle of the Bulge and that some German commandos were captured and shot while wearing American uniforms.

Nat's letter of December 31, 1944, to his Mom and Dad was written from Belgium. He had this to say about the events of the past two weeks:

"I know you have worried about me for not writing but as you can readily see by the country (Belgium) I'm now in and the news on the radio I know you will understand. Weather has been very cold. Have plenty of ice now. Spent Christmas at the front. Had our Xmas dinner today and are going to have turkey again tomorrow for New Year's. It was really good. Received a swell picture of Fran (Nat's wife) and the baby in a little wallet like form. They are really beautiful. I'm a lucky guy. Hope you had a nice Xmas. Will write more later."

Little did Nat know that this would be the last letter he would write to his Mom and Dad until January 24, 1945, because of his being wounded on January 4, 1945. The events that followed are described below.

NAT IS WOUNDED ON JANUARY 4, 1945, AND IS SENT TO AN ARMY HOSPITAL IN ENGLAND FOR RECUPERATION (JANUARY 4 TO MARCH 15, 1945)

On January 3, 1945, the Allied Forces were going all out to exploit the Bulge and push the Germans back into Germany.

"But the weather was foul: subfreezing temperatures, heavy overcast, icy roads, fog, drifting snow. The Germans, fighting a skillful withdrawing action, were shrewd in their resistance. It was slow going. Too slow." (General Bradley, p. 385)

On January 3, 1945, Nat's unit, Company E, 66th Armored Regiment, was assigned to 2nd Armored Division's Combat Command A Task Force Bravo. At 8:30 A.M., Task Force Bravo attacked to take the high ground east of Magoster, Belgium. This took about 30 minutes, and the Task Force assumed a defensive posture by 10:15 A.M. His company was now about 1,200 yards northwest of Devantave, Belgium and reported 10 enemy tanks in the town. It called for air support, but none was available because of poor flying weather. Artillery fire was then called on to shell the town. At 2:00 P.M., Task Force Bravo was ordered to resume the attack to capture Devantave, but received heavy shelling from German heavy tanks, artillery, and automatic weapons from the vicinity of Consy. At 6:40 P.M., the "criminal type, ratty, young, and tough" Germans of the 2nd SS Panzer Division launched a combined tank-infantry counterattack from woods west of Devantave but were repulsed by Task Force Bravo's tanks and supporting artillery. Task Force Bravo consolidated its position for the night after advancing only about 2,000 yards this day. (Houston, pp. 357, 359)

This was the situation that Nat found himself in during the early morning hours the next day on a bitterly cold, snowy, foggy January 4, 1945. There were icy roads like regular toboggan slides that reminded him of Lewis Run, and snow about knee-deep near Devantave, Belgium.

Around 4:50 A.M., the Germans launched the first of their three counterattacks made during the early morning hours of January 4, 1945, to drive Task Force Bravo from the vicinity of Devantave. The other two counterattacks occurred at 6:15 A.M. and 8:30 A.M. All three were repulsed by American artillery shells with variable time fuses that exploded over the German soldiers and equipment spreading shrapnel over a wide area with deadly effect. (Houston, p. 359)

It was during this second counterattack that Nat was wounded while standing in his tank's turret on guard duty. He described this situation in his January 27, 1945, letter to his Mom and Dad, written from the 4149th U.S. Army Hospital in England:

> "I was *injured* [italics mine] the morning of January 4th at about 7 o'clock. It was snowing very hard…With visibility very limited, I suddenly spotted two large tanks moving up and across our front about 400 yards away. I got out of the tank to remove the snow from the gunner's sights, and immediately they were blurred again. The gunner fired and missed. Before he could fire again, I saw a flash and then something hit me in the face…the Jerry (GI's nickname for a German) was a bad shot. The armored piercing shell just hit the top

of the tank and hit three hand grenades on the turret. The hot armored piercing shell whizzed past my left ear. I was very lucky. The pieces (fragments from the exploding hand grenades) made a big hole in my tank helmet (made of cloth and not of steel) but I had only a small hole in the top of my head. Other small pieces hit me in the forehead and one small piece in each eye. The pieces in my forehead are coming out gradually. My left eye just had a little piece in it and my right one had to be cut a little. It just missed my pupil but did not hurt my vision one bit."

Nat learned later that his "gunner knocked out the Mark III tank that shot at us. We now have two (tanks) to our credit, two half-tracks, and we didn't stop to count the dead Krauts (Germans)." (Nat's January 24, 1945, letter to his Mom and Dad)

When the grenades exploded, the blast blew off his helmet and his head was bleeding. He was also temporarily blinded in both eyes by the shrapnel. He bailed out of the tank and ran aimlessly down the hill until he was picked up by his medics. They placed him in a litter basket on the side of a tank and transported him to his Battalion Aid Station.

"Put yourself in the wounded guy's shoes when he sees the medic appear over him, and his pain has been dulled by morphine, his bleeding is stopped, and he is lifted out and carried back to safety and good surgery. Sure, he's going to love that medic. And after a few dozen men owe their lives to one man, that little pill roller is going to be very well-liked indeed." (Mauldin, p. 121)

Nat was then evacuated immediately to a military hospital in Paris to remove the shrapnel. He was now no longer a "fighting soldier" but a "helpless patient." He got some consolation in knowing that 95% of wounded soldiers survived if they got to a military hospital. He was at different hospitals in France for 19 days.

He was blind in both eyes for 18 days. The doctors put magnets over his eyes and forehead to pull out fragments. In his letter of January 24, 1945, to his parents, he wrote:

"Sorry I haven't written sooner but I have been moving from one hospital to another. I am fine and can see perfect. I arrived here in England yesterday after a boat and train ride from France. Wrote to Fran a couple of times and know she called you. Please use my old address as they will forward it here. I am convalescing and will go back to my outfit from here. I have been resting very well and eating OK. The weather is a little cool. There is a little snow here. There sure was plenty in Belgium. The morning I got hit it was really coming down."

Then on January 27, 1945, he wrote to his parents:

> "I read the eye chart perfectly yesterday. It (his right eye) is healing fine and I am not having any trouble at all."

According to his sister, Louise, Nat's parents were notified sometime in the middle of January 1945 of his being wounded. She recalled that she saw an Army sedan parked in front of their house. There was a knock on the door. She answered it and was met by two soldiers who asked, "Is this where Mr. and Mrs. Humbert Piscitelli live?" She replied, "Yes." One of the soldiers then told her that Nat was wounded. Louise exclaimed, "Oh, my God!" and called her mother, who screamed, "Dio Mio! (Oh, my God!)." They called Nat's father, and all three blessed themselves. The two soldiers then departed.

Nat's wife, Fran, who was staying with her mother in Louisville, KY, was also notified by a soldier coming to her home. She knew immediately that something was wrong. He told her that Nat had been wounded and was recuperating in a hospital in England. She recalls that she was eating bacon* and feeding small pieces to her eight-month-old daughter, who was sitting in her highchair when the soldier arrived. She was shocked to hear the news. She also received a telegram from the War Department notifying her that Nat was wounded. She phoned this information to Nat's parents. Neither Fran nor Nat's family knew the nature and severity of his wounds until his first letters started to arrive in late January and early February 1945.

(*Note: Bacon was rationed during WWII, so Frances enjoyed the one pound she was able to get each month. Sugar, coffee, shoes, nylon stockings, tires, and gasoline were also rationed.)

Nat's brother, Clem, was now a Master Sergeant and stationed in the Adjutant General Section at Base "F" in New Guinea. Because of the time it took the Army to notify his parents that Nat had been wounded and because of the two to three weeks it took a letter to get from the States to New Guinea, Clem was not aware that his brother was wounded and in an Army hospital in England. In Clem's letters to his parents from January 5 through February 4, 1945, he was concerned about Nat because he knew the 2nd Armored Division was involved in the "Battle of the Bulge." Clem wrote:

> "January 5, 1945 (One day after Nat was wounded): Pleased to know that you are getting mail from Nat & that he is well & safe—pray that it remains that way for always & that he gets relieved soon."

"January 29, 1945 (Nat was now in an Army hospital in England): Pleased to hear that Naz is well that he is OK."

"February 4, 1945 (Nat was in an Army hospital in England): Do you hear often from Naz & Frank (Clem's brother in the Army Air Corps stationed in La Junta, CO) lately? Pray that all is well. I imagine Naz is having it pretty tough but I'm sure with our Lord's help all will turn out OK."

Clem finally got word that Nat was wounded and recovering when he received a letter from his family in the middle of February 1945.

Nat was one of the 48,000 Americans wounded during the Battle of the Bulge. In addition, there were an estimated 8,000 killed and 21,000 captured or missing in action—for a total of 77,000 men. Also, there were 733 U.S. tank and tank destroyer losses. (General Eisenhower, p. 365)

In Nat's January 27, 1945 letter to his parents, he wrote:

"Remember the Lieutenant I used to drive for, he got hit the day before I did. An artillery shell went right in the turret. The outcome was something awful. I have had three close calls and I think my prayers have helped more than once."

Nat recuperated for the next two months at the 4149th U.S. Army Hospital in Cirencester, England. He required six (6) eye operations. On January 27, 1945, he was presented the Purple Heart Medal at a ceremony held in the Hospital's chapel. He sent the medal to his wife.

Nat was treated well during his hospital stay. The food was good, except when being served fish for breakfast from time-to-time. He was able to attend movies at the Hospital's Recreation Center. On February 7, 1945, he wrote to his Mom and Dad that he had seen "Dragon Seed" with Walter Houston and Katherine Hepburn about the Chinese people's war with the Japanese. He also reported seeing "Home in Indiana" about horse racing. He also got a four-hour pass to the nearby small town which he reported as having "a beautiful theatre and a few pubs" where he could get a taste of the English beer again.

While Nat was in the hospital, his nephew and sister Fannie's son, Staff Sgt. Joseph (Joe) M. Ross, Jr., was stationed in the 8th Air Force in England as a gunner on a U.S. Army Air Corps B-17 bomber. On February 16, 1945, Nat wrote to his parents:

"Would like to have Joseph's address so I could write him a few lines and probably get a chance to visit him or he could write me."

Then in Joe's March 27, 1945 letter to Nat's parents, i.e., Joe's grandparents, Joe wrote:

"Presume you've heard of my fortunate completion of my missions. Was hoping to contact Naz, but without success. Haven't given up yet but I doubt very much if it's possible as I'll be leaving soon."

Nat and Joe never did meet while they were both in England.

(Note: Joe completed 36 bomber missions over Germany in less than three months and was now eligible to rotate back to the States. For him to have survived 36 B-17 bomber missions without being shot down was why he used the word 'fortunate' in his letter. Very few bomber crew members were that lucky since three out of four were either killed, wounded, or missing. After the war, Joe was a successful accountant in Pennsylvania and Florida. Joe died on July 16, 2001, at the age of 75. The author documented Joe's WWII memoirs in 2000.)

However, while in the hospital, Nat met other patients from Pennsylvania. One was Joe Garpetti from Erie, PA. Joe was married and was on his way back to the States as he was wounded in the leg and throat and lost his voice. Nat wrote that Joe's wife may call Nat's mom and dad.

(Note: On June 21, 2002, while working on this story, the author, and his grandson, Quinn, met with 89-year-old Joe Garpetti and his wife at their home in Erie, PA. Joe was an assistant gunner in Company A, 644th Tank Destroyer Battalion. Like Nat, he was wounded during the Battle of the Bulge and was the only member of his 5-man crew who survived a direct hit by a German 88mm shell. His tank commander was hit in the head and died in Joe's arms. The death of his crew members is still hard on Joe because they had been together for over two years. He didn't remember Nat; however, Joe was eager to talk about his medical treatment. He spent 18 months recovering in hospitals in England and in the United States for wounds suffered to his eyes, throat, arm, hands, and legs. He still has trouble talking because of his throat wound and is classified as 98% disabled by the U.S Veterans Administration. He is very proud of his unit and of his service to his country.)

As of February 7, 1945, Nat still hadn't received any mail. However, he still wrote V-Mail letters almost daily to his wife and his parents. He also wrote many letters to his family members, relatives, and friends. This shows that Nat was a very caring person and was endeared to all who knew him and cared about him. He maintained these traits all throughout his life.

In his letter of February 13, 1945, Nat wrote to his parents:

> "Friday (February 10, 1945) made three years I've been
> in the Army. It means I start drawing longevity pay
> an increase of $4.85 per month." *(Underline added.)*

(Author's Note: Nat was now authorized to wear a "hash
mark" on the left sleeve of his uniform denoting his three
years of service.)

> "The weather has been terrible here, rain and more rain.
> I'll let you know as soon as I leave here. Wednesday
> (February 15, 1945) starts another Lenten Season. I
> hope I'll be home at this time next year."

In his February 16, 1945 letter to his Mom and Dad, Nat wrote
that he still hadn't received any mail and there just wasn't
anything to write about. However, he did comment that:

> "War news sounds good in the Pacific but the floods* are
> holding up the boys here. I hope it won't be too long."

(*Note: These floods were caused by the spring thaws and by
water releases when the Germans destroyed the discharge
valves on two Roer River dams.)

Then in his February 20, 1945 letter to his parents, Nat addressed these areas of his life that meant a lot to him:

"Another dehydrated letter to tell you I am fine and just about ready to hit the road again.

"Today is Peggy Anne's birthday (his 9-month-old daughter he has never seen). I'll bet she really is quite a beauty. I hope it won't be too long before I can see her. I really am missing the best part of her life now, but I'll pay up for it when I come home. She's going to get the best of everything and really have a chance in life. I'll bet Fran spends most of the day getting her all prettied up. Damn this old war.

"Haven't received any mail yet but sure wish I could get some soon. When a guy doesn't receive mail, he just isn't himself. When I do receive some it'll probably be about twenty or twenty-five at one time."

Finally, in his letter of February 22, 1945, he wrote that he had received his first mail, which took only 18 days to get to him from Pennsylvania to England.

"Dear Mom and Dad,

Your letter of Feb 4th made me very happy. It was the only letter I received. I was glad to hear that Fran called when she received the telegram (War Department's notification that he had been wounded) and when she received my first mail. I should be receiving mail quite regular now.

"I know how worried you were Mom, but you can forget all about it now because I am fine and in the pink of condition. Tell everyone thanks for asking about me and coming to see you. Sorry to hear that Matt (Langianese) and Johnny (Pingie) have not written. I know Johnny was near me but I don't know about Matt.

"I'll send you the doctor's certificate as soon as I am discharged. It shouldn't be too long now. I sure hope this war ends soon…"

Then on March 6, 1945, he wrote that his mail was finally catching up with him. As he predicted in one of his earlier letters, he received 20 letters in one day. Most were from his wife, Fran (who wrote to him every day), from two of his sisters, Fannie and Louise, who also wrote the V-Mail letters for his parents who knew how to write in Italian but had trouble writing in English, and from two of his brothers, Frank, who was a Corporal in the Army Air Corps in Arizona and Clem, who was a Master Sergeant in the Army in New Guinea in the South Pacific. Clem was planning to marry a girl he met while serving in Australia. Nat wrote: "It is too bad that he may not be able to go through with his marriage as planned."

As it turned out, Clem, who had been in the South Pacific for almost three years, was given a 45-day leave back to the States in April-May 1945. While on leave, Clem, his sister, Vera, and sister-in-law, Faye Piscitelli, went to Louisville, KY to visit Nat's wife, Fran, and her baby. This time, they could fly, rather than take the train, because the Bradford-McKean County Airport was completed during WWII. The only problem was that Vera and Faye were bumped off the plane in Cincinnati, Ohio to give their seats to servicemen. Here is what Clem wrote on a postcard to the author, his nephew, about this trip:

"April 20, 1945: Hi Mate: Having a good time. A swell place here. See you soon. Hello to all. Cobber, Clem"

He particularly enjoyed going to a night club in Louisville, the Club Madrid, and finding out what comforts he missed while being in the South Pacific.

Then, here is what Vera and Faye wrote on their postcards to the Costanzo Family:

"April 20, 1945: Hello Everyone, Am having a grand time. Enjoyed the plane ride very much. See you soon. Love, Vera & Clem"

"April 21, 1945: Hello Everyone, Flying is sure the only way to travel. Perhaps after the war we can charter a plane, and all go to Ky (Kentucky) that way. Love, Faye"

Nat continued to express his concern about the status of his hometown friends, Matt and Johnny, because neither he nor their families had heard from them since the Battle of the Bulge. He thought they were now somewhere in Germany near the Rhine River. He commented that "Hope this damn war ends soon. We still have a tough fight ahead of us."

(Note: Both Matt Langianese and Johnny Pingie survived the Battle of the Bulge and the rest of the war. However, one of Nat's friends from Lewis Run, PA, Charlie Fair, was killed during the Battle of the Bulge.)

NAT RETURNS TO HIS UNIT FOR THEIR FINAL THRUST ACROSS GERMANY (MARCH 17 TO MAY 7, 1945)

In early March 1945, Nat's vision in both eyes recovered, even though his left eye was slightly blurred. He was then released from the hospital and was sent to a nearby Replacement Depot in England. He thought he was returning to the States;

however, this was not what the Army had in mind as he now found himself on the way back to the war now raging inside the German Homeland.

> When a soldier gets out of an army hospital, he will most likely be thrown into a 'repple depple.' This institution, identified in army regulations as a replacement depot, is a sort of clearinghouse through which soldiers who have been separated from their outfits or soldiers newly arrived from the States have to pass for reassignment." (Mauldin, p. 122)

This is exactly what happened to Nat as he described it in his March 15, 1945 letter to his parents:

> "I just wrote to Fran and told her how mad I was. I told her about leaving the hospital marked limited-service* and when I arrived here (Replacement Depot in England) they changed their minds and are sending me back to the outfit. Maybe the war will be over with by time I get back. Sometimes I get so disgusted I don't care what happens. Oh well, such is life.

> "I have been waiting around to get processed, paid, etc. Just like getting inducted all over again. I'm fine and getting plenty to eat. The weather has been beautiful which helps out a lot especially having to wait in

chow lines, pay lines and P.X. lines. Boy, I never saw so many guys coming back from different hospitals. I met only one guy I knew back in the states. He used to work in the motor pool at Knox."

(*Note: It was not unusual in World War II to be in the service if your disability was having good vision in only one eye. In fact, Nat's brother, Frank, who completely lost the sight in one eye during his early childhood and replaced it with a glass eye, was drafted into the Army in 1942 and served with the Army Air Corps in the United States until he was honorably discharged in 1946. After the war ended and Nat was back in the States and now a civilian, his vision from his left eye deteriorated. He completely lost the sight from his left eye as a result of his wounds. In 2002, he had 20/25 vision in his right eye, the one that was operated on in France in 1945. Then, when he had a cataract removed from that eye, the doctor found a hole in its pupil. Even in 2002, some 58 years after he was wounded, he still had shrapnel being removed from his head.)

Nat again crossed the English Channel by ship for the third time. He entered Germany by way of Holland, where he had been in August-September 1944. On April 1, 1945, while in Holland, he wrote this to his parents:

"Easter Sunday. Went to Mass and Communion this morning. It isn't too good outside but I guess there won't be any Easter Parade here. I am in Holland again and on my way back to my outfit. Should be with them in a few days. I'm fine, so please don't worry.

"Observed the Holy Week nicely and am ready to start the second half of the big drive to Berlin. I am confident the Good Lord will watch over me and send me home safely to you, Fran, and the baby. Sorry I haven't written too often but you can understand the circumstances moving from one place to another. We are quartered in a fairly nice building which has a few shell holes in it but as long as we are kept dry, I guess we can be thankful."

While at a Replacement Depot in Germany, Nat wrote on April 6, 1945, that they were being housed in buildings, rather than in tents, only a few miles from his old outfit.

"We spend a few hours marching and the rest of the time is spent playing games if possible. I went to Church last nite. We had very nice services in an old schoolhouse. I met quite a few boys from the Second Arm'd. I hope the same old gang is still together...We have been having a lot of fun from playing cards and talking about the different outfits."

In addition, when Nat had time to chat with his buddies, the conversations generally turned to these subjects:

> "...no matter how many of his friends may come to shoot the breeze with him, there are only a few subjects of conversation: wives and girls and families, just plain women, or home." (Mauldin, p. 158)

In early April 1945, Nat rejoined his old unit, which was now in Germany between the Rhine and Elbe Rivers, pursuing the retreating Germans and pushing to link up with the Soviet forces. He was one of the 3,063 members of the 2nd Armored Division who were returned to duty after being either injured or wounded. (Houston, p. 439)

Nat was again assigned as a tank commander, but with a new "green" tank crew who had just arrived from the United States. Because there had been so many casualties among tank crews, replacements were rushed from basic training in the States directly to the frontline units. Most of them were 18-19 years old. The normal procedure was to assign a least one seasoned combat veteran with each tank crew. Hence, Nat fit that category and again found himself in the role of instructor—responsible for training a crew as he did while serving at the Armored Training Center at Fort Knox in 1942, 1943, and part of 1944. Except now, he had to do it under combat conditions.

The 2nd Armored Division was now near Magdeburg, Germany, on the Elbe River, having come 226 miles in 19 days after crossing the Rhine River. They secured a bridgehead on the east side of the Elbe on April 12-13, 1945, but abandoned it under fierce German resistance on April 14, 1945. The U.S. Army Ninth Army Commander, General Simpson, wanted to launch an attack across the Elbe and capture Berlin. However, he was overruled by General Bradley who felt that the military didn't have the supplies (gas, ammo, bridging) and believed it would suffer 100,000 casualties. General Eisenhower then made the final decision to let the Russians get Berlin. (General Bradley, pp. 424, 427, 428)

It was on April 12, 1945, that President Franklin D. Roosevelt (FDR) died at Warm Springs, Georgia of a massive cerebral hemorrhage at the age of 63. Nat recalls that, when the troops were given the news, most of them cried over the loss of their President. They were not sure what the death of FDR would mean for the war in Europe, except maybe for them to fight a little harder to honor him and to give him the high praise he rightly deserved. (Irwin, page 128) President Roosevelt's last words that he dictated before he died are a tribute to his legacy: "The only limit to our realization of tomorrow will be our doubts of today. Let us move forward with strong and active faith." (Henry F. Groff, *The Presidents*, p. 440) FDR was succeeded by his Vice President, Harry S. Truman.

The 2nd Armored Division successfully assaulted Magdeburg with the 30th Infantry Division on April 17-18, 1945. The division then moved to the occupation zone south of Braunschweig, Germany on April 20, 1945, and mopped up German stragglers in Forest Konoigslutter on April 21-22, 1945. Nat's crew was assigned guard duty during this time. Tension mounted as no one wanted to become a casualty during the last days of the war.

The war in Europe ended officially on May 8, 1945, and was known as "V-E (Victory in Europe) Day." Nat reported that most of the American soldiers celebrated by getting drunk on good German beer, or on homemade American whiskey called "White Lightning," or on wine called "Vino."

Nat did not meet any Russian soldiers. He was told about the German concentration camps and the atrocities after the war was over. He did not visit any of the camps.

EPILOGUE OF THE
2ND ARMORED DIVISION

Out of a possible 335 combat days from June 6, 1944 (D-Day) to May 7, 1945, the 2nd Armored Division entered combat on July 2, 1944, and was in action for 223 days (66% of the time). It sustained 6,751 battle casualties (killed, wounded, and missing) and 7,116 non-battle casualties for a total of 13,867. The division's turnover rate of personnel was 95%, meaning that the division, with a required strength of 14,460 personnel, had, by V-E Day, basically all new people from when it first entered combat on July 2, 1944. For the most part, the composition of the 2nd Armored on V-E Day was from men who had been stateside during D-Day. (Ambrose, pp. 283, 288)

"The 2nd Armored Division is justly proud of its history, written across two continents (Africa and Europe) through blazing sun, rain, fog, and snow. Its professional performances revealed an aggressive determination and desire to be a great combat team. Attacking across mud and through snow, it has written its story in blood, sweat, and tears. Bravery was the only accepted standard; often deeds of valor were rewarded with less than the merited decoration. For thirty months, the division fought, and its battle history reveals that once it started toward greatness, it continued until it had attained that status. The 2nd Armored Division epitomized armor warfare during World War II and demonstrated convincingly that it was second to none." (Houston, pp. 433, 434)

NAT'S ROLE IN THE ARMY OF OCCUPATION IN GERMANY (MAY 8 TO SEPTEMBER 30, 1945)

After the war ended, Nat's unit was initially on occupation duty in Germany. He was in the American Sector established at the Yalta Conference five months before the war ended. His daily routine consisted mainly of guard duty. On May 12, 1945, the 2nd Armored Division was relieved of its occupation duty and assigned the mission of setting up a staging area in Bienrode, Germany. Afterward, it began its mission to be the first American division to enter and guard the American Sector of Berlin. The division entered Berlin on July 4, 1945, following a 48-gun salute. (Houston, pp. 424, 425)

One of Nat's fondest memories during this time was in mid-July 1945 when the Big Three—President Truman, British Prime Minister Churchill, and Russian Premier Stalin—met in Potsdam, a suburb of Berlin, to discuss matters relating to postwar Europe and the war in the Pacific. The 2nd Armored Division units served as President Truman's honor guard and conducted a military review with their vehicles—tanks, artillery pieces, etc.—on display along the German Autobahn* for inspection by the visiting dignitaries. Nat's tank crew, along with all the other crews in the division, rubbed diesel oil on the outside of their tanks to make them shine in the sun. He was most impressed when he saw his division in a line stretching for miles. He now appreciated what it took to defeat the German war machine that had overrun most of Europe in 1939 and 1940 and the tremendous job that the Allied forces had done to accomplish this difficult task.

(*Note: The autobahns were built by Hitler in the 1930s as a massive public works project to help solve his unemployment problem. These "super" highways also gave him the capability to move his army rapidly to all parts of Germany. Once the motorized and armored units of the U.S. Army crossed the Rhine River, they used the autobahns to enhance their speed and mobility to overrun German units and to capture thousands of prisoners. Some U. S. soldiers called the autobahns "Hitler's tombstone—one foot thick and a thousand miles long.")

The 2nd Armored Division started to leave Berlin on August 6, 1945, to a new location in Germany. Nat described the move in his August 12, 1945 letter to his parents, written from Gelnhausen, Germany.

"We left Berlin August 6 on Monday morning at 3:30 A.M. We traveled 125 miles that day on Hitler's great autobahn (built by Hitler for the rapid movement of military equipment). We slept in pup-tents. That nite it rained cats and dogs. The next morning we got up at 3:30 and left at 5:00 A.M. We traveled 125 miles that day and bivouacked near Kassel at 6:00 P.M. in the evening. We left again in the morning at 6:30 A.M. and traveled about 90 miles to a town by the name of Lieblos about 32 miles from Frankfurt. We parked our tanks on an abandoned airfield and pitched pup tents in a straight line. There were over 2000 tents. There were over 4000 soldiers in the Area.

"For exactly two days and a half, it rained so damn hard that the water seeped in under the tents. Boy, were we a mess. Yesterday we moved about four miles into some old German Barracks which were bombed. They are in a hell of a shape. They leak and we have no hot water."

While on occupation duty, Nat was offered a commission as a 2nd Lieutenant by his Company Commander if he volunteered to fight in the war that was still going on against Japan. He turned it down because he was sick of the war, sick of the Army, and just wanted to go home to be with his family, especially the daughter he had never seen.

In early August 1945, the two atomic bombs were dropped over Japan. In his August 12, 1945 letter from Gelnhausen, Germany, Nat commented:

"The news is now on and they say everyone is waiting for the news of Japs Surrender. I hope they do surrender. If they don't, we will wipe them off the face of the earth. Boy, that Atomic Bomb must be something."

The war with Japan ended on August 15, 1945, and was called V-J (Victory in Japan) Day. It was a great day for the men of "Hell on Wheels," not just for Nat and his unit, but for the entire world. Most of the soldiers celebrated by getting drunk as they did after V-E Day in May 1945. In his August 18, 1945 letter, Nat wrote:

> "The news of the war being over was really swell. We had our radio on all nite and waited for the news. At 1:10 A.M. we heard that the war was over with. I was too excited about it. I just rolled over and went back to sleep. The boys with less than 85 points were really happy. They thought they would have to go to the Pacific."

After the war in Europe ended, General Eisenhower had over 3,000,000 Americans under his command. He had to devise a scheme for assigning men with the longest battle service to German occupation duty or to be sent back to the States. Others were to be transferred to continue the war in the Pacific as the United States needed additional manpower as it prepared to invade the Japanese Home Islands. The scheme was called the "point system" and was based on "credits for length of service, length of time overseas, decorations, parenthood, and age." (General Eisenhower, p. 430)

Nat's letter of August 12, 1945, was the first to his parents addressing the "point system." He had 98 points consisting mainly of one point for each month he served in the Army, one point for each month he served overseas, five points for each of his five battle stars, and five points for each of his five decorations/medals. He also got some points for being married and having a child and for his age; however, he liked to say he didn't get any for being "handsome." He wrote:

> "We are expected to leave here (Gelnhausen, Germany) in a few days, that is men with over 85 points. We are going to either the 5th or 7th Armored Div. and then home. I figure that I should be home Sept. 15th or the later part of Sept."

Then two days later, in a letter he wrote to his Mom and Dad at 2:30 A.M. on August 14, 1945, he said:

> "I am O.K. and still sweating out the point system. They are down to 105 points now, so it shouldn't be too long."

Implementing this system required many manpower transfers from veteran divisions and filling these vacancies with men with less battle service.

"Application of the system was tedious, but probably no better plan could have been devised to accommodate the conflicting considerations of fairness to the individual and the efficiency of units. An added difficulty arose when the War Department found it advisable to change the 'critical point' score. This created additional work, to say nothing of confusion and some discontent." (General Eisenhower, p. 430)

However, in his next letter to his parents, Nat became one of General Eisenhower's "discontents." Nat expressed it this way in his August 18, 1945 letter:

"We were all set to transfer to the 12th A.D. (Armored Division) when the war ended. Now everything has been changed and we won't leave until Sept. or October. Boy, I'm so dammed mad I could scream. Those 98 points of mine are like 40 now. I'm not doing a damn bit of work. I'm just lying around taking it easy. Tomorrow another buddy and an officer are planning to go to Mannheim to play a little golf...They aren't sending anyone home from here...Last year at this time I was with the division 5 days and fighting like hell in France. Now I am in Germany and just sitting on my a_ _. Ah! Ah! You know what I mean.

"Glad to hear you received the pictures I sent. I don't see where I got fatter. I'm not too anxious about getting out of my Army clothes. I just want to get home. Who knows, if they give a big enough bonus I may reenlist. Oh yeah! Glad to hear you called Fran. I know she was happy to hear from you all. Believe it or not Mom, she hasn't missed a day of writing except when she came home (Lewis Run, PA) on vacation and was kept busy visiting everyone. Boy, she sure is one swell wife."

Then, Nat wrote this on August 23, 1945, from Aschwege, Germany and still assigned to Company E, 66th Armored Regiment:

"Got transferred to the 5th Armd. Division today. Please stop writing. We are expected to arrive in the States around Sept. 23rd if there are no change in plans. Everything looks fine. Get out the spaghetti and chicken, also Budweiser out of the icebox."

Finally, on September 9, 1945, Nat left Germany and was located at Camp Atlanta, France where he was assigned to Service Company, 10th Tank Battalion. Things were looking up as he wrote:

"I'm fine but very excited about coming home. Things have been happening fast. We will leave here for

LeHavre, France about Wednesday. Then we may have to go to England to get one of the big Queen boats ("Queen Mary" and "Queen Elizabeth" were British luxury ocean liners being used as troopships with each accommodating over 8,000 troops). These are the latest rumors. That means we will set sail about Sept. 27th and arrive home in October. It makes me so damn mad. If we didn't go to Berlin, we would be civilians today."

While Nat was at Camp Atlanta, France, he met another of his friends and a neighbor from Lewis Run, PA, Aldo Zandi. In his September 9, 1945 letter, he wrote to his parents:

"I gave Aldo Zandi a big surprise today. He is at Camp New Orleans about 3 miles from me. I kept his address from the paper (*The Bradford Era*) and had no trouble finding him. We were together for six hours. He got very fat and is looking fine. We had chicken for supper too. We talked about old times. Tell Mrs. Zandi that he is fine and that he may be home for Xmas, who knows. It sure was swell seeing him."

Nat's enthusiasm was short-lived because on September 21, 1945, Nat was still in France, but now at Camp Twenty Grand*. He was one "upset soldier" as he wrote:

"It is just a month since I left the 2nd Armd. Div. and this is the farthest I've gotten to. According to the schedule, I should be a civilian this very minute. I hope to hell I never had left the 2nd. So do a lot of other boys. Two boys wrote cablegrams to Senator Wheeler, Senator Luce, and another one asking why men with 106 to 91 points are still sweating it out over here and living in a hell hole like this camp. There is a line everywhere you go here. You even have to stand in line to take a shit. Excuse the language please.

"The P.W. (Prisoners of War) do all the work here, washing, K.P. (Kitchen Police), cleaning up, etc. Boy, are they nice and healthy. They even drive trucks. I imagine they'll be pulling guard next.

"We got some straight dope for a change and now we are supposed to leave Tuesday, Sept. 25th. Which means that we should be in the States about Oct. 1st or 2nd. I hope I'm pretty sure I'll go to the Indiantown Gap Separation Center (Pennsylvania).

"I've tried to forget all I've been through, but I still have trouble sleeping at night."

(*Note: Embarkation camps for soldiers departing from Europe were named for cigarette brands included in GI rations. Camp

Twenty Grand was on the rocky ground overlooking the Seine River in France. Camp Lucky Strike was also a large embarkation camp in France.) (Gerard, page 307)

However, he was still upbeat, as he continued:

> "Tell everyone hello, Mom. I don't want you to go through a lot of monkey business when I get home. Just plain cooking like you always do and some good old Budweiser beer if you can.

> "Love Always,
> Your Son, Nat
> XXXXX
> Five extra for a good gal
> XXXXX"

V. RETURN TO THE STATES

(SEPTEMBER 30, 1945 TO OCTOBER 21, 1945)
TRIP HOME FROM FRANCE

(SEPTEMBER 30, 1945 TO OCTOBER 8, 1945)

N at finally departed from France on September 30, 1945, on a converted Liberty troopship. Even though the ship was, as he described, "a bucket of bolts" and not one of the luxury liners he had hoped for, the morale, food, and accommodations on this ship were better than the one he first boarded to England in May 1944. He landed in New York and, as he expected, arrived at Camp Indiantown Gap, PA on October 8, 1945.

DISCHARGE FROM THE U.S. ARMY
(OCTOBER 8-21, 1945)

By the time he arrived at Camp Indiantown Gap, PA, he now earned 114 points and was selected for discharge. He was one of approximately 8,250,000 men and women serving in the United States Army.

So, on October 21, 1945, and without much fanfare, he was given an Honorable Discharge as a Staff Sergeant. After more than three and one-half years in the U.S. Army, Nat was a civilian again. He received some back pay plus $200.00 mustering out pay, and a gold-plated, diamond-shaped lapel button called a "Ruptured Duck" because it was "in the form of an eagle that looked more like a duck." The button was given to all discharged service personnel who had served honorably in the Armed Forces in World War II.

Nat's brother, Steve, met him when he arrived home in Lewis Run, PA. But Nat was drunk from having celebrated his discharge, so it took Steve and several others to pick him up. His parents did have that big meal ready for him and the Budweiser as he requested.

His brother, Clem, who had been home on a 45-day leave in April through May 1945 from Southeast Asia, was discharged as a Master Sergeant in June 1945 at Fort Dix, NJ because he had 90 points. Consequently, he did not have to report back to his unit in New Guinea even though the war with Japan did not end until August 1945.

Nat's other brother, Frank, was now a Sergeant in the Army Air Corps in Bakersfield, CA. He was discharged in January 1946, having served the duration plus six months because he did not have the required 85 points for earlier discharge.

Everything was OK for now. He had proved himself, did his job fighting for his country, and survived. He was now back in his hometown of Lewis Run, PA—a tiny piece of American democracy with only 800 people sitting along both sides of US Highway 219. Nat was welcomed home by his neighbors and friends of many nationalities, but all were Americans. He was proud to be one of three stars on the small flag hanging in the window of his parents' home to show that they had three sons serving in WWII. All that was left for Nat to do now was to rejoin his wife, Fran, in Louisville, KY and to see and to hold his seventeen-month old daughter, Peggy Anne, for the first time.

Fran kept Nat's picture in Peggy Anne's playpen during the entire time he was away. She did this in hopes that his daughter would recognize him when he finally got home. Being away from his first-born child was the hardest and worst part of the war for Nat. Fran picked him up at the Louisville train station and took him home. He was sitting in the living room when Peggy Anne ran into the room. She looked at him and said, "Hi, Daddy!"

AWARDS AND DECORATIONS

Nat's brother, Clem, in his job in the Army in New Guinea as a Master Sergeant processing personnel records, had this to say in a letter to his parents on January 21, 1945 about awards.

"Just received the Era (the Bradford, PA hometown newspaper) stating that Johnny Pingie (also in the 2nd Armored Division with Nat) was awarded the Bronze Star. He did a wonderful thing but knowing awards & seeing other fellows commended & awarded medals, he certainly deserved more than that, I know because I see a lot come through. It sure is too bad, but the main thing is that he is OK and that counts most of all."

Nat's awards and decorations for his three and one-half years of military service include:

1. Purple Heart for being wounded in action on January 4, 1945.

2. Bronze Star Medal for Valor for calling in fire on a concentration of German soldiers. (He was using a pair of captured German binoculars at the time because they were more powerful than his GI Issued pair.)

3. Bronze Star Medal with Oak Leaf Cluster for another incident involving combat with the enemy.

4. Good Conduct Medal for being an exceptional soldier with an unblemished record during all his military service.

5. Distinguished Unit Citation for the 2nd Battalion, 66th Armored Regiment's action on July 26 to August 12, 1944, preparatory to and during the advance of the 2nd Armored Division from the general vicinity of St. Lo to the Argentan-Falaise pocket.

6. European-African-Middle Eastern Theater Campaign Medal (EAME) with five Battle Stars for serving in five European campaigns (Normandy: June 6 to July 24, 1944; Northern France: July 25 to September 14, 1944; Rhineland: September 15, 1944 to March 21, 1945; Ardennes-Alsace: December 16, 1944 to January 25, 1945; and Central Europe: March 22 to May 11, 1945).

7. Belgian Croix de Guerre Decoration for liberating Belgium. Nat recalls that a very impressive ceremony was held in Germany shortly after V-E Day when the Belgian dignitaries presented this medal for the first time to an entire foreign military force. All the 2nd Armored Division units were in the parade while aircraft flew overhead. (Houston, page 424)

8. Belgian Fourageres (shoulder braid) for liberating Belgium. This braid is worn on the shoulder of the uniform.

9. Two Overseas or "Hershey" bars for serving more than 12 months overseas in a hostile fire zone (one for every six months of overseas service). They are worn on the right sleeve of the uniform. "Hershey" is a WWII designation referring to Louis B. Hershey, who was the Selective Service Director.

VI. NAT'S REFLECTIONS ON FIGHTING A WAR

"For all we have and are,
For all our children's fate,
Stand up and meet the war.
The Hun is at the gate!
Our world has passed away
In wantonness o'erthrown.
There is nothing left today
But steel and fire and stone."

"For All We Have We Are"
(Rudyard Kipling)

UNIT'S COMBAT PERFORMANCE

"In general, in assessing the motivation of the GIs, there is agreement that patriotism or any other form of realism had little if anything to do with it. The GIs fought because they had to. What held them together was not country and flag, but unit cohesion." (Ambrose, p. 473)

Nat agrees that everyone in his unit just wanted to defeat the Germans as quickly as possible and go home. They lived and fought as a unit because their survival depended upon each other.

Even though his unit saw a lot of combat, Nat did not recall any incidents where anyone in his company suffered from "shell shock" or "combat fatigue" (sometimes called "battle exhaustion"). If they had, then they would find themselves trembling constantly and had to be evacuated to the rear for treatment. They would have to be treated like any wounded or injured casualties, requiring extensive physical and emotional recovery.

COMMENTS ON THE M4 SHERMAN MAIN BATTLE TANK VS. GERMAN TIGER AND PANTHER TANKS

In his book, *Death Traps*, Benton Y. Cooper, a World War II Ordnance Liaison Officer with Nat's sister heavy division, the 3rd Armored, claims that one of the greatest tragedies of World War II was that the U.S. Armored troops had to fight the Germans with inferior 32-ton M4 Sherman main battle tanks. He reached this conclusion because the U.S. Army tanks lacked the firepower, armor, and mobility of the heavier German Mark IV, Mark V Panther, and Mark VI Tiger tanks. The latter weighed 70 tons and was called "King Tiger" and seemed almost invincible. The Germans first used it in the Battle of the Bulge and created a "Tiger Phobia" reputation that panicked some of the American troops, especially when they saw its gun which was the size of a large and long telephone pole. (Cooper, p. 213) (*History Channel*, "Tiger Attack," January 13, 2002)

A Sherman tank could usually be knocked out by a single shot from a German 75mm or 88mm tank or anti-tank guns with their high velocity, armor-piercing rounds. Unless shots fired by a Sherman hit a German tank on its rear side, the German tank could remain in action. The Sherman tank also caught fire too easily because it was fueled with gasoline rather than diesel as used in German tanks. (Cooper, p. 213)

Nat and his crew compensated for these shortcomings by doing the best with what they had. They learned how to use their tanks to achieve maximum effectiveness against the German tank and anti-tank weapons and equipment. If their tank didn't have enough armor to stop a German 88mm high-velocity shell or a round from a German anti-tank gun, they added to their tank's hull in strategic places: sandbags, spare track blocks, wooden timbers, and logs laced with chicken wire, angle iron, and even in some cases concrete. If their tank was getting stuck in the mud, they widened its tracks to 20-inches by bolting "duck feet"—3-inch wide steel grousers to each track block on both sides. However, the German tank tracks were 30 to 36 inches wide, which still gave them better traction in soft, wet ground. When the roads got covered with snow and ice, his crew could get one-half-inch square steel blocks, about two inches long, welded to the bottom of the wedge screw on the track connector to better penetrate ice and hard-packed snow. (Cooper, pp. 90, 140, 141, 158)

On the other hand, the Sherman's power traverse turret was a distinct advantage. It was "faster than hell." A Sherman crew could get off two or more shots against a German tank before the German crew could get its turret's gun around to fire at the Sherman. The Sherman tank also had a gyro-stabilized gun control to enable the tank's crew to fire its main gun while moving and still have the gun remain fairly level. Even though the Sherman had this feature, Captain Cooper states that the tank crews appeared hesitant to use it and preferred to fire from a stationary position. (Cooper, pp. 213, 238)

In addition, the Sherman tank was:

> "...built around a Ford engine, which could be removed and replaced with a spare in a few minutes...it was comfortable to live in...In the spaces between the ammunition they (the crew) stowed socks, sleeping bags, letters from home, and all the canned food, tea (British crews), coffee (for U.S. crews) and cigarettes that smooth talk and light fingers could win from the lines of supply...when the ground was dry enough to assure that the tracks would not sink during

the night, they would sleep under it in the summer."
(Keegan, p. 197)

Nat said that the German soldiers were very good and well trained, especially their tank (Panzer) crews. These crews had been fighting since 1939 in Poland, Africa, and Russia. They were "...trained not to think about their weaknesses but only about their superiority." (Irwin, page 137) Also, the German 88mm tank gun and the Tiger and Panther tanks were far superior to our 75mm and 76mm guns on our Sherman tanks.

It has been said that it took five of our Sherman tanks to knock out one German tank. We had this advantage in numbers because America's "Arsenal of Democracy" harnessed the mass production capabilities of the U.S. automotive industry and produced 48,000 Sherman tanks in WWII. This was twice the number of German tanks. So, while German tanks were superior, there were a lot more U.S. tanks to shoot at them. Although the U.S. forces had this numerical advantage, its tank crews paid a heavy price in casualties. It is unfortunate that they, like Nat's tank crew, had to fight the Germans with our inferior tanks. The American tank crews fought the good fight with their weapons and equipment. (*History Channel*, "Patton and the Sherman Tank," September 25, 2000)

It wasn't until late February 1945 that some U.S armored units were issued for combat testing 20-experimental T26

Pershing tanks. These tanks weighed 43 tons and had 4-1/2 inches of armor plate as compared to the Sherman's 32 tons and 2-1/2 inches of armor plate. The Pershing was mounted with a 90mm gun compared with the Sherman's 76mm gun. At a range of 1,000 yards, the Pershing tank's gun proved that it could penetrate any German tank's thick side armor. A platoon of Pershing tanks was first on the scene to help secure the Ludendorff Railroad Bridge at Remagen, Germany over the Rhine River. Nat was not issued a Pershing tank, but was a tank commander initially with an M4 Sherman with its 75mm gun and then later with an M4A3 Jumbo with its 76mm gun. (U.S. Army in World War II, *ETO—The Last Offensive*, pp. 169, 212)

A tank's tracks are supported by a series of steel rollers, called "bogie wheels." The Dresser Company in Bradford, PA was one of the U.S. companies that manufactured "bogies" during WWII. Nat's oldest brother, Jim, worked for this company. Who knows if Nat may have been riding on some of the "bogies" produced by his brother?

NAT'S "ALMOST" COURT MARTIAL INCIDENT

Nat likes to recall how he almost got court-martialed when he used his 76mm tank gun to fire at some German troops. Nat's commanders felt that if you wounded more of the enemy than you killed, then the enemy would have to use more of their personnel to take care of the wounded than to bury the dead. Consequently, they would then have less of their personnel available to fight. Therefore, his orders were that his tank's gun was not to be used to fire on troop concentrations. That was a job for the artillery or the tank's machine gun if the troops were in range. After firing his tank's gun, Nat saw the bodies of German troops flying in the air when his shell hit them. That gave him some satisfaction to atone for the number of U.S. servicemen he had seen killed or wounded. Since it was unclear as to whether or not he killed any of the enemy, as opposed to wounding them, there was no action taken against him.

SABOTAGING HIS TANK'S ENGINE

Nat also recalled that once he and his crew sabotaged their tank's engine so that they could get three days of rest while the engine was being replaced by a tank maintenance unit. This occurred after they had been in continuous contact with the enemy for many days without any relief. The crew felt they had been "pressing their luck," and they might be the next tank to be destroyed by the Germans.

QUALITY OF SUPPORT FROM OTHER U.S. UNITS

Nat got very good support from the engineer, infantry, artillery, maintenance, and medical units attached to his battalion. He especially appreciated the air support from the P-47 "Thunderbolt" and P-38 "Lightning" fighter-bombers of the U.S. Army Air Corps.

DAILY HYGIENE

Since they were always moving and water was scarce, Nat and his crew would wash and shave whenever they could find water. Most of the time, most bathing was done using their helmets as washbasins. Helmets proved to be a valued piece of equipment to the soldiers. They used it to dig with and to cook in it.

For a tank crew member, the steel helmet was also a convenient, portable urinal and toilet if you couldn't leave the tank. There was no problem finding a convenient place to "dump" the contents outside the tank, even if the tank was moving. (Irwin, p. 41)

Nat would shave with cold water about once a week. In all of his years overseas, he doesn't ever remember taking a shower. He was issued free toilet articles by the Army whenever he was fortunate enough to come across a supply station. They were called "PX" rations and consisted of soap, shaving cream, razor blades, and aftershave lotion.

If combat soldiers were able to take a hot shower, it was generally a makeshift affair in the middle of the field set up by the Army's Quartermaster troops. The soldiers would find three canvas enclosures, each topped by a homemade water tank being fed by a hose hooked to a gasoline pump set up by a nearby creek or pond. The water was heated with gas heaters. Twenty (20) naked men at a time would be assigned to a shower which, by this time, the areas both inside and outside of it were ankle-deep in mud. So, before they showered, the mud provided a great opportunity to engage in another type of battle—a "mud fight." They would have one minute to get wet, then the shower would be turned off as they took the next minute to lather if they could find a cake of soap in the mud. The shower would then be turned back on, and the third minute would be for rinsing. Then it was outside walking in the mud and in the chill air to let the cold air dry them off as there were no towels! They got dressed in a hurry putting on any clean clothes if they had any! (Irwin, pp. 149, 150)

FOOD

Nat's basic food while in combat consisted of "K-rations." The meal was pre-packed in a small paraffin-coated waterproof paper* box. For breakfast, the box consisted of a small can of scrambled eggs and bacon pressed into a patty. Lunch (dinner) was a can of cheddar cheese, and supper was a can of potted meat much like today's canned Spam. All the cans were about the same size as a small can of today's tuna fish.

All the meals contained high protein Waverley crackers. There were also packets of coffee, powdered lemonade or orange-ade, powdered milk, sugar, cigarettes, matches, chewing gum (mainly Chiclets and Dentyne brands), and toilet paper in each box. Most importantly, each box contained a small can opener, which was affectionately named a "P-38" after one of the U.S. World War II fighter bombers.

(*Note: Plastic packaging material didn't become available until after WWII.)

In situations when these rations were not available, Nat was issued "C-rations." These were an individual serving of a 12-ounce tin can of 10 different meat combinations; for example, meat and vegetable stew, pork and beans, or meat and vegetable hash. With each of these cans, he was issued a separate 12-ounce size can of condiments consisting of three hard biscuits, three pieces of hard candy, one small can of preserves, two sugar cubes, and one packet of soluble coffee. (*War Department Pamphlet 21-13*, "Army Life," pp. 59-62)

From time-to-time, he might be issued a "10-N-1 ration." This ration allegedly contained enough food and condiments to feed two soldiers for five days. It included two types of canned meat—Spam and corned beef. The rations also came with canned green vegetables, canned fruit, crackers, coffee, toilet paper, and cigarettes. (Cooper, p. 63)

Nat agrees with Mauldin who wrote about K and C rations:

"I suppose they had all the necessary calories and vita-
mins, but they didn't fill your stomach and you got
awfully tired of them." (Mauldin, p. 171)

Nat's emergency ration was a high protein chocolate bar with
bran flakes, called a "D" bar. The "D" didn't stand for "delicious" because it was hard as a rock and took about half an
hour to chew it. Nat would sometimes give the chocolate bar
to the local French and Belgium citizens who in return gave
the American soldiers flowers and Cognac.

While engaged in combat, Nat was seldom served a hot meal.
However, when his unit was in reserve, the company cooks did
prepare some hot meals. His crew would occasionally supplement their diet with meat, fruit, and vegetables scrounged
from the French, Belgium, Dutch, or German countryside.

Like Mauldin, Nat liked to think of scrounging like the borrow-
ing of things which make life in the field a little more bearable.

Nat wrote about scrounging for fresh vegetables in his August
12, 1945 letter to his Mom and Dad.

"We didn't get any chow but "C" rations, so some of
the boys went out and shot a cow, stole corn and dug

up some potatoes. We had steak for two meals and ended the (meat) with hamburgers tonite. Boy, it was really swell. We are getting good chow now."

Earlier, while at a Replacement Depot in Holland on April 1, 1945, he wrote:

"Boy, I've had more fresh eggs this week than I can count. They were really good too. We don't get eggs too often so one appreciates them when he does get a few."

Nat always looked forward to supplementing his diet with food packages from his wife, parents, other relatives, and friends. In his letter of December 11, 1944, he wrote to his Mom and Dad:

"Your package of Sept. 22nd (took 11 weeks to reach him) also came today. The pepperoni, fruit cake, cookies, and candy all came in fine condition. Thanks very much. I sure appreciated the pepperoni. The fruit cake lasted about ten minutes. The boys really enjoyed it. Then another of the crew got two packages and they both had fruit cakes in them."

Nat was especially grateful whenever he received his Mom's glass jars of meatballs and her pizzelles (a traditional Italian waffle cookie), as well as his sister's (Fannie) glass jars of chicken soup. Since styrofoam and other plastic packaging materials weren't on the market until after WWII, the jars were surrounded with cotton and then packed and mailed in tin coffee cans. His wife, Fran, kept him supplied regularly with olives, fruit cake, deviled ham, and cookies.

He also got packages from the Red Cross, along with coffee and donuts. He still hasn't forgiven the Red Cross for charging front line soldiers 10 cents for a donut. The soldiers thought the donuts should be free considering all that they were sacrificing for the war. Nat didn't know that the federal government mandated the Red Cross to charge troops for coffee and doughnuts.

The cigarettes in Army rations came four to a package. They were the popular brands of the day. They were even packaged with brand names and advertisements printed on the packages.

Nat was one of the few soldiers in the U.S. Army who didn't smoke, so he would give his cigarettes to his Army friends who did. When asked why he didn't smoke, he related this story.

"When I was 12 years old, I and my hometown friend, Mike "Friday" Ross, got a hold of a carton of cigarettes. We went under the bridge near Ross's Store in Lewis Run and started to smoke them one after another. Eventually, I got sick to my stomach. I stopped smoking and went home "sick as a dog." I told my Mother that I was ill because I had eaten green apples. She believed me. I never smoked another cigarette after that day."

CLOTHING

Nat's clothing consisted of a woolen shirt, woolen trousers, long underwear tops and bottoms. He had no daily change of clothing, except maybe for clean socks once every few days. He also had a pair of tanker coveralls, a tanker jacket, tanker boots, and a tanker's padded leather helmet. He managed to clean off the grease from his clothes with gasoline about once every other day. He was seldom issued a complete change of clothing. From time-to-time, he would receive socks and undershirts sent to him by his relatives. He would also wear his steel helmet for added protection while engaged with the enemy.

SHELTER

Most of the time while in actual combat, Nat would sleep in his bedroll next to or under his tank. Occasionally, if he were lucky, he would take shelter in an abandoned building, provided it was first cleared of any mines and booby traps.

REST AND RECREATION (R&R)

After about one month in combat, Nat and his crew were generally granted three days of leave at an R&R Center run by the Army. He did not see any USO shows. The USO shows were staged to let the servicemen and women know that they hadn't been forgotten by the people back home. They were designed to give the audience a few hours of happiness and fun. However, Nat's brother, Clem, stationed in New Guinea, did comment on this USO show in his letter to his parents on January 12, 1945:

> "Just returned from the stage show "Cover Girls Abroad." One of the best Army stage shows I've seen. Had 4 of Harry Conover's Cover Girls—3 girl acrobats—a singer, drummer & dancer. About an hour-long but real entertainment. Sure was good to see an evening gown again, especially on a cover girl. One of the girl's name was Candy Jones whose picture has been on most of the magazine covers. Really swell—chalk up a point for the U.S.O."

Nat was able to read the Army's daily, four-page news publication, *Stars and Stripes*, occasionally. This newspaper carried:

> "...the latest U.S. news, sports, and commentary, as well as poems, stories, articles, and cartoons produced by U.S. troops. At times, pinup girls graced its pages.

Gen. George C. Marshall called it 'a symbol of the things we are fighting to preserve...free thought and free expression of a free people.'" (Fredericksburg, VA, *Free Lance Star*, July 20, 2002)

Bill Mauldin's "Willie and Joe" cartoons appeared in *Stars and Stripes.*

In 1942, the U.S. Army started to publish a weekly magazine called *Yank*, written by and for American service personnel. Its staff was enlisted personnel to give it a "Dogface to Dogface" approach. It covered hometown and humorous stories. It graced its pages with "pin-up" pictures. George Baker's "Sad Sack" cartoons were also featured. Stories about the antics of the officers in the service were "fair game" for its enlisted writers. There were no ads in it. It cost 5 cents and had 2 million subscribers for its 21 different editions. The magazine was phased out when the war ended in 1945. (*History Channel*, "Color of War," May 13, 2003)

MAIL (BEFORE E-MAIL THERE WAS V-MAIL!)

Most of the letter mail sent from the States and from overseas was called V-Mail and was developed by the British in 1942. An individual (civilian or military) would write the letter on a special 8-1/2" x 11" form which would be folded to become its own envelope. This form would then be mailed to an Army Post Office in the States or overseas where it would be photographed on microfilm and the film shipped to its destination. There the microfilm would be processed to produce a small 4-1/4" x 5-1/4" print and sent to the addressee. This was done to save space and weight in transporting the 65 million letters written on the average in one month by both the servicemen/women and the people at home to be sent across the oceans from or to the States. By using the V-Mail method, 1.5 tons of letters could be reduced to 45 pounds. Nat called a V-Mail a "dehydrated" letter. He and other servicemen wrote on average of six letters a week. (*History Channel*, "Dear Home: Letters from WWII," June 7, 2002)

Service personnel in WWII could mail their letter and postcards without any postage provided they wrote "Free" in the stamp's location. Nat took full advantage of this privilege. Letters written by Nat and other service members were read and stamped by a censoring officer to make certain that no locations, unit designations, and movement orders were included. This practice was stopped shortly after the end of the war in Europe.

There was a "Mail Call" for Nat's unit about three to four times a week. This was always the highlight of the day for him as any news from home was welcome. Mail was Nat's connection to home and normal life. It allowed him to keep up with the growth of his newborn daughter. Just like any first-time dad, he was excited about his baby even though he didn't see her for the first time until she was seventeen months old.

As mail call was the highlight of army life, not receiving mail left a soldier crestfallen. In his February 20, 1945 letter to his parents, over a month and a half since he was wounded and while he was convalescing in the Army hospital in England, he wrote:

> "Haven't received any mail yet but sure wish I could get some. When a guy doesn't receive mail, he just isn't himself. When I do receive some it'll probably be about twenty or twenty-five at one time. Say hello to all and please don't worry. Love Always, Your Son, Nat"

Nat would write letters to his wife, his parents, the rest of his family, and friends whenever he had a lull in the fighting. They were all censored by an officer before he could mail them "Free." As seen from his letters quoted here, he wrote about what he had been through, what might happen to him next, and sometimes what might lie ahead for him in the distant future. He did his best to keep them informed without worrying them. But war being what it is, this was hard to do.

Nat would receive letters and packages from home on an irregular basis even though his wife, Fran, wrote to him every day. Also, his sisters, Fannie and Louise, wrote several times a week, most of the time for his parents, who could write in Italian but not in English. His sisters also were writing their parent's letters to Nat's other brothers in the service—Frank, stationed in Colorado/Arizona, and Clem, in Australia/New Guinea. His other family members, including some of his nieces and nephews, wrote to him on a regular basis.

He particularly enjoyed receiving letters from his oldest sister, Fannie, because she was up on all the gossip concerning most everyone who lived in Lewis Run. In his August 18, 1945 letter to his Mom and Dad, Nat wrote:

> "Tell Fannie to give me the latest dope. Her last issue of the "Scandal Sheet" hasn't arrived yet."

RELIGIOUS SERVICES

While in combat, he was not able to attend Catholic Mass or any other religious service on a regular basis because he was too busy fighting. His battalion chaplain would visit Nat's unit from time-to-time. While Nat was recuperating in the hospital in England, there was always a Chaplain available. The Chaplain was a good person to contact if he had any personal problems.

Nat attended services whenever he had the opportunity. He had then and continued to have strong religious beliefs that got him through many difficult situations during the war, as shown in some of his previous letters included here. He had this to say in a letter to his parents on August 14, 1945, while stationed in Gelnhausen, Germany:

> "Went to Mass Sunday and went again last nite [sic] to Parent's Mass which is held every Monday if possible. They have a swell Church and our Army Chaplain is very nice."

PERSONNEL IN NAT'S UNIT

The members of Nat's platoon (30-50 men) and company (150-200 men) were from various parts of the United States, with most of them being from Illinois, New York, and New Jersey. When the war ended in Europe on May 8, 1945, Nat recalls only one member of his platoon remaining from those in it when he first joined the unit in June 1944. He is still in contact with one of the other tank commanders, Glennon Rathgeb, from Carlinville, IL. Glenn also saw action with the 2nd Armored Division in North Africa and Sicily.

PAY AND ALLOWANCES

"Army pay must be thought of at all times in terms of the extras which go with it. Not only are America's fighting men better paid than others, but they receive the best living quarters available, good clothing and excellent food, medical and dental care, certain tax exemptions, allowances for dependents, debt relief, and free entertainment and recreation." ("Army Life," p. 18)

Nat's base pay when he enlisted was $21.00 a month. He sent $15.00 to his Mother and kept $6.00 for spending money. His Sergeant's base pay was $78.00 a month. After he was married, he sent an allotment of $43.00 to his wife and kept $6.00 for spending money. After he reached three years of service, he received a 5% longevity pay increase of $4.85 per month to his Staff Sergeant's base pay of $96.00 per month. His overseas pay was 20% of his base pay for an additional amount of $19.20. His total monthly pay while overseas was $120.05. When the war ended, a Private's monthly base pay was now $52.50, while a Brigadier General's (one star) was $660.60 a month. For comparison purposes, the base pay for a recruit in the 2019 U.S. Army is $1,680.90 per month. (www. goarmy.com)

WAR SOUVENIRS

Nat had a pair of German binoculars, a German Luger pistol, a German SS storm coat, and a German camera. He took the Luger off a dead German that he came across. He confiscated the others in a house that had been occupied by the Germans. He kept the German camera. He used the binoculars to look for enemy targets as they were more powerful than those issued to him. The SS storm coat was stolen while he was on the ship coming home. He thinks his brother, Jim, may have kept the Luger pistol.

FRENCH PEOPLE

"The French were honestly and sincerely glad to see the Americans come, and the further north (from the U.S. landings in Southern France) we were the more hospitable the people became. I had a feeling that we were regarded truly as liberators, and not as walking bread baskets." (Mauldin, p. 204)

While moving through France, he saw the French people stoning the women who had collaborated with the Germans during the German occupation of France.

GERMAN PEOPLE

Nat did not have much contact with the Germans. However, he did know that the Germans would pay $100.00 for a carton of American cigarettes.

VII. NAT'S LIFE AFTER HIS MILITARY DISCHARGE

Nat's wife, Frances (also called "Fran"), and daughter, Peggy Anne, stayed in Louisville, KY with his wife's mother while Nat was overseas. Frances worked at Brown-Forman Distillers as Secretary to the Vice-President before she got married. Her mother helped care for the baby. After his discharge, Nat joined Frances and the baby in Louisville, KY. They stayed there for one month before moving to Lewis Run, PA. Nat recalls seeing his former girlfriend, who lived next door to his parents' house, standing on her front porch crying when he brought his family home.

Nat and his family initially stayed with his parents in Lewis Run, PA. Fran, being an only child, was awed by the size of the Piscitelli family. She recalls cooking the 1945 Thanksgiving dinner for 26 people from Nat's family. It was a gargantuan task!

Then in 1946, they bought a house on Oxford Street in nearby Bradford, PA. Their first son, Nat, "Sonny," was born on August 21, 1946, also their third wedding anniversary.

Nat needed a job to support his family. He could have joined the "52-20 Club" until he found a job and received unemployment benefits of $20.00 a week for 52 weeks as provided for in the GI Bill of Rights (Servicemen's Readjustment Act). However, he went to work right away for the Tuna Manufacturing Company as an Apprentice Cabinet Maker under the GI Bill. He took night classes and finished his apprenticeship in three years. Nat was paid $1.75 an hour. The U.S. Government gave him $90.00 a month and paid for his tools as part of his education benefits earned under the GI Bill. It was ironic that his brother, Frank, who also had sight in only one eye, worked for the same company after he was discharged from the Army Air Corps. The saying around town was that "It took one eye from each of two brothers to make the best cabinets in town."

Frances was an accomplished dressmaker. She helped to support the family by making wedding gowns, school uniforms, and dresses.

Nat worked at Tuna Manufacturing Company until 1951. After spending many cold winters in Pennsylvania and remembering his miserable days with the snow and ice in Europe's 1944-45 winter, he and Frances decided to move to California. They sold their house on Oxford Street for $16,000 for a nice profit from the original $9,700.

He and Frances then went to Michigan and purchased a new 1951 Dodge car and a 35-foot trailer and still had $2,000 left in cash. Father Kennedy, the Lewis Run pastor, blessed the trailer while it was parked by Leone's Store. The last thing loaded on the trailer was Frances' sewing machine. They and their two children left Bradford, PA in October 1951 for the Big West. Relatives could see the car and trailer as it traveled on US 219 and waved at them until it got out of sight. They later learned that the sewing machine fell off while the car and trailer were traveling up a hill. It took them 21 days to drive through many states before ending their trip in Stockton, CA. Nat recalls that it took them five miserable days just to travel through Texas. Only Nat's sister, Fannie, knew they were expecting their third child when they left Bradford, PA.

Nat got a job right away at American Forest Products where he was hired to use an electric screwdriver to screw hinges on ammunition boxes to support the Korean War effort now underway. His pay was still $1.75 an hour just as it was at Tuna Manufacturing Company. He held this job for a few weeks and then drove his trailer and moved his family to Tracy, CA— twenty miles away. He then went to work from 1951-1955 as a cabinet maker for Wood Products, Inc. for $2.00 an hour. Their second son, Anthony Christopher, was born on April

9, 1952. Their second daughter, Theresa Marie, was born on August 25, 1953.

While living in Tracy, CA, they found their trailer to be too small to house their growing family. However, they were fortunate that there was a woman in Tracy, CA who wanted to sell her three-bedroom, one-bath house to live in a trailer. Nat and Frances made the $4,000 down payment for the house by using their trailer, which they had purchased for $3,500.

It was tough for Nat and Fran during their early years in California. With their growing family of four, a house to pay for and steady jobs hard to come by, Nat had to take any odd job that he could find to make ends meet. Even if it meant traveling long distances. Fran also took in sewing to help.

While working in the cabinet shop, Nat learned that there was a minimum-security prison in Tracy looking for a person to teach hobby woodworking at night. He took the job in 1955. In the meantime, the instructor in the prison's cabinet shop was retiring, and the State of California was advertising the job. Nat took the test, was Number 2 on the list of applicants, was interviewed, and got the job after the Number 1 candidate declined the job because he didn't want to move.

Because Nat had no teaching experience, he had to attend classes at the University of California in Berkeley to earn his teaching certificate. He went for four summer sessions during his vacation time in July and August. This was a tough time for him because he was involved with classes from 6:00 A.M. to noon. He would then drive to the prison and teach from 1:00 P.M. to 5:00 P.M. But all this effort was worthwhile because Nat received his teaching credentials. He was now able to teach in any public school and in any state or federal institution. He and his family then decided to move back to Stockton in 1959 and lived in the same house for the rest of their lives.

While teaching cabinet making at the Deuel Vocational Institute, Nat had twenty inmates in class, usually six African Americans, eight Hispanics, and six Caucasians. He taught them how to use hand tools and machines to become cabinet makers. Some of the inmates learned the trade, but others just "did their time." There was no prison guard with him, and the door to the shop was always locked. Nat felt it was almost like being inside his tank again and getting shot at. This was not a pleasant situation for him to be in, but just like during the war, he learned to live with it.

He recalls only one incident when he felt threatened. In 1960, the inmates planned to simultaneously take as hostages all twenty-two instructors in each of their separate shops. Nat's students were the only ones who implemented the plan. As soon as the inmates found out that the other prisoners had not gone through with the plan, the class released him.

When Nat's mother died on July 30, 1960, at the age of 72, he took his first airplane flight to attend her funeral. He remembers it as a breathtaking experience as the propeller-driven plane flew through a violent thunderstorm over Missouri. He said there were lightning flashes all around the plane. He was scared to death when he saw sparks coming from the plane's engine. It was more harrowing to him than anything he ever experienced in his tank battles. On the morning of the funeral, Nat passed out when he saw his mother's body. He was admitted to the Bradford hospital for several days due to chest pains. After that experience, he never returned to Pennsylvania for any funerals, including that for his father who died on January 15, 1974, at the age of 88.

In the summer of 1961, Nat recalls that his sister, Vincie, his brother-in-law, "Barb," and their daughter, Theresa, visited them. They traveled by train from Pennsylvania to California. He drove them in his two-door Pontiac to Joe DiMaggio's Restaurant at Fisherman's Wharf in San Francisco, CA and through the vineyards in the Delta Area of California.

Nat worked at the Prison for 18 years until 1973 when he was retired on Industrial Disability. His blood pressure reached 210/160, and he had a partial stroke but recovered. He then went to work as a customer service representative for a home building contractor. His job was to make sure all construction met the building codes and that all appliances were in good working order. He performed this job for one year and then moved to another company for more pay. Here he worked as a carpenter doing fine finishing work in homes. He left this job in 1981. He then went on his own doing finishing work and installing hardware, crown molding, and Formica tops. At the age of 82 years old he was still doing this type of work at least four hours a day. His loss of vision in his left eye from his war wounds did not hurt his ability to do fine finish carpentry work.

In 1983, to celebrate their 40th anniversary, Nat and Frances went on a tour of Europe. They visited 30 cities in 30 days. Aachen, Germany was one of the cities they visited. This is the place where Nat's tank was hit in the fighting in January 1945.

Nat's car license plate shows that he is a Purple Heart recipient. Strangers would come up to him, shake his hand, and thank him for serving his country. He also flew the U.S. flag every day at his house.

Nat and Frances enjoyed life watching their four children grow up and having successful careers and families of their own. They still called on their Dad whenever they needed his carpentry expertise.

As far as anyone in their family pursuing a military career, their son, Sonny, served for 25 years in the U.S. Air Force as a missile specialist and retired as a Captain. He also served a tour in Vietnam. One of their grandsons, Scott, served a tour in the U.S. Marine Corps. Another grandson, Brian, graduated from the U.S. Air Force Academy in 2003 and trained as an F15-E Strike Eagle jet pilot.

Nat continued to maintain a very close relationship with his brothers and sisters. Even though they live on the East Coast and him on the West Coast, he found time to phone or visit them or to go East periodically to attend the Annual Piscitelli Family Reunion in Pennsylvania, which has been held every year since 1947. Here's how Nat's niece, Anne Piscitelli, describes what the reunions meant to her as mentioned in the book about the history of the Grilli and Carrara families:

> "Childhood summers we would go to Lewis Run for the Piscitelli Reunion usually held on the 4th of July. Always 80 plus people. Was always great to see and meet and watch cousins, aunts and uncles grow and mature as I did. This experience gave me a great understanding and respect for 'family values'."

At the most recent family reunion in 2019, it was announced that there are now 483 Piscitelli family members who are the result of the union between Humbert and Anna.

VIII. CONCLUSION

Nat Piscitelli was a true "citizen-soldier" in every sense. When his country called, he answered. He then fought for his country to the best of his ability, survived, helped to win victory in Europe, and then returned home to take up being a dedicated husband, father, son, and citizen again.

This account is by no means the whole story of Nat's military service in World War II and his civilian life after it was over. It only recreates those significant events that made a lasting impression on him from the time he first enlisted until more than three and one-half years later when he was honorably discharged and those events associated with rebuilding his life after he came home.

Nat was one of many tank commanders who had the safety and the welfare of his crew foremost in his mind. He always did the best he could with the equipment that he had. There is no better testimony as to his performance and to his character than that given by Glennon Rathgeb, one of the soldiers who served with the 2nd Armored Division in Africa, Sicily, and Europe and then in Nat's company in Europe. Glennon had this to say in his letter to the author on November 10, 2000 (some 56 years after he first met Nat):

> "In answer to your letter about Nat and the war, I can tell you that your uncle was a very good soldier and friend. We enjoyed a lot of good times together and a lot of hell up on the line. Their tanks were not better than ours, but their 88mm gun had us outranged by better than 1,000 yards. The difference was the men, like your uncle. We all could use our own brains. I send cards to Nat, Harold Cary, and Chick Cherril. They are the only ones that I know who are alive. You can well be proud of your uncle. He was always there when needed and did a super job." (Letter from Glennon Rathgeb, November 10, 2000)

Then Nat, as a civilian again and as a husband and parent, used his wartime experiences to help him serve his family and community to the best of his ability. He did not let his war wounds take over his life. He made the most of his physical disability to become an accomplished cabinet maker, prison instructor, and carpenter. Through all this, he maintained his personal values of responsibility, duty, honor, and faith. He was never afraid to recall his combat experiences to get them "off his chest" and to talk about them.

Nat is one of the many Americans, cited in President John F. Kennedy's January 20, 1961, inaugural address, who has lived up to all that is expected of any citizen of this great nation, both in war and in peace.

"The torch has been passed to a new generation of Americans born in this century, tempered by war, disciplined by a hard and bitter peace, proud of our heritage" (and bid his fellow Americans) "Ask not what your country can do for you. Ask what you can do for your country."

IX. ABOUT THE AUTHOR

Colonel Albert C. Costanzo, U.S. Army (Retired) is Nat Piscitelli's nephew. His mother is Nat's sister, Vincie. Al grew up with his uncle in Lewis Run, PA, and corresponded with him during World War II. When Al returned from the Korean War in November 1953, Nat met him and welcomed him home when Al's troopship arrived at the Oakland Army Terminal, CA.

Al was drafted into the Army in July 1945 at the age of 18 just before the end of WW II. He attained the rank of Corporal as a surveyor in the U.S. Army Air Corps and was stationed in Texas, Washington State, Colorado, Florida, and New York State. In 1947, he received an appointment from the Army to attend the U.S. Military Academy at West Point, NY. Al graduated from West Point in June 1951 as a 2nd Lieutenant in the U.S. Army Corps of Engineers. During the next 30 years, he served in various engineer assignments in the Korean War, the Vietnam War, Western Germany, and the United States (Pennsylvania, Massachusetts, New York State, Kansas,

North Carolina, and Virginia—including three tours in the Pentagon). He retired in 1981 as a Colonel with 36 years of service. For several years, he documented World War II experiences of his relatives.

He and his wife, Rose (also from Lewis Run, PA) have six children (five sons and a daughter) and nine grandchildren. They made their home on a Christmas tree farm in Culpeper County, VA, were volunteer tutors for the Culpeper Literacy Council, and were both involved with making quilts.

Of their five sons: their oldest spent three years in the U.S. Army as a photographer in the United States and Germany. He also served several years with a U.S. Air Force Reserve unit in Chicago as a Master Sergeant until his unit was disbanded. Two sons have pursued military careers in the Virginia National Guard. Two other sons are civilians working for the Department of the Army. Their one and only daughter has two young sons who enjoy playing with their "GI Joe's" and other military-type toys.

Colonel Albert C. Costanzo
U.S. Army (Retired)
(Uncle "Naz's" Nephew)

ALBERT C. COSTANZO

Passed away on October 5, 2011—Age 84

X. SOURCES

1. During period 1998-2002:
    a. Questionnaires prepared by Author and completed by Nat
    b. Personal Interviews with Nat by Author and Author's Sister
    c. Correspondence between Author and Nat
    d. Telephone Conversations between Author and Nat
    e. Interviews with Nat's brothers and sisters by Author
    f. Taped Interview of Nat and Frances conducted by their daughter, Peggy Anne, in November 2002

2. Nat's letters to his parents and family, 1942-1945

3. Nat's 2nd Armored Division WWII Album and Historic Report

4. October-November 2000 Correspondence between Author and Glennon Rathgeb, who served with Nat in the 2nd Armored Division

5. Ambrose, Stephen E., *Citizen Soldiers: The U.S. Army from the Normandy Beaches to the Bulge to the Surrender of Germany, June 7, 1944 to May 7, 1945*, New York, Simon and Schuster, 1998.

6. Bradley, General Omar, *A Soldier's Story*, New York, Simon and Schuster, 1951.

7. Brokaw, Tom, *The Greatest Generation*, New York, Random House, 2001.

8. Cooper, Belton Y., *Death Traps: The Survival of an American Armored Division in World War II*, New York, Random House, 1998.

9. Crow, Duncan and Icks, Robert, *Encyclopedia of Tanks*, New Jersey, Chartwell Books, 1975.

10. Eisenhower, General Dwight D., *Crusade in Europe*, New York, Doubleday, 1948.

11. Eisenhower, David, *Eisenhower at War 1943-1945*, New York, Random House, 1986.

12. Gerard, Philip, *Secret Soldiers: The Story of World War II's Heroic Army of Deception*, New York, Dutton, 2002.

13. Graff, Henry F., *The Presidents: A Reference History, New York,* Scribner, 1984.

14. History Channel Episodes:
    a. "D-Day-Breakout," September 13, 2001
    b. "Dear Home: Letters from WWII," June 7, 2002
    c. "High Tech Weapons-Tanks," July 20, 2002
    d. "Patton and the Sherman Tank," September 25, 2000
    e. "Sherman Tanks," May 01, 2002
    f. "Suicide Missions: Tank Crews," December 17, 2000
    g. "Tiger Attack," January 13, 2002
    h. "Tiger Tanks," July 14, 2002

15. Houston, Donald E., *Hell on Wheels, The 2nd Armored Division*, New York, Presidio Press, 1977.

16. Irwin, John P., *Another River, Another Town: A Teenage Tank Gunner Comes of Age in Combat-1945,* New York, Random House, 2002.

17. Jones, James, *WWII*, New York, Grosset and Dunlap, 1975.

18. Martin, Ralph G., *The GI War 1941-1945*, New York, Little Brown, 1967.

19. Mauldin, Bill, *Up Front*, New York, W.W. Norton & Co., 1945.

20. 20. MacDonald, Charles B., *The U.S. Army in World War II-The Last Offensive*, Atlanta, GA, Whitman, Reissued 2012.

21. Neidich, Joyce Grill, *The Descendants of the Grill(i) and Carrara Families of Pettorano Sul Gizio, Italy, Volume III*, Apollo, PA, Closson Press, 1995.

22. Scales, Jr., General Robert H., *Certain Victory: The US Army in the Gulf War*, Dulles, VA, Potomac Books, Inc., 1998.

23. Stanton, Shelby L., *World War II Order of Battle: An Encyclopedic Reference to U.S. Army Ground Forces from Battalion through Division, 1939-1946*, Mechanicsburg, PA, Stackpole Books, 1984.

24. United States Military Academy, *The War in Western Europe, Part 2, (December 1944 to May 1945)*, New York, USMA, 1949.

25. *War Department Pamphlet 21-13*, "Army Life", Washington, D.C., 1944.

XI. PHOTOS

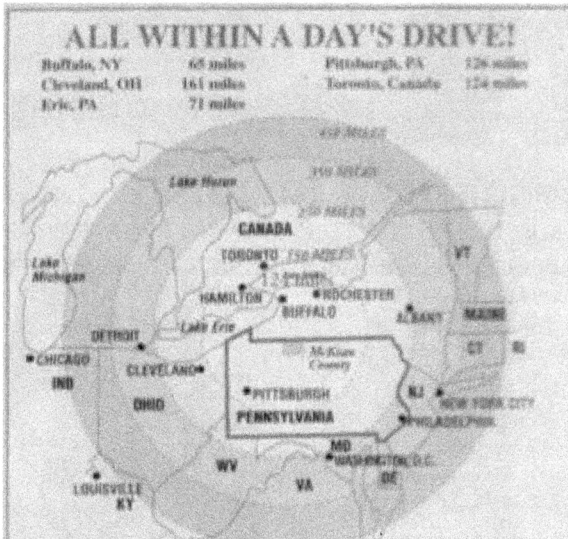

ALL WITHIN A DAY'S DRIVE!

Buffalo, NY	65 miles	Pittsburgh, PA	126 miles
Cleveland, OH	161 miles	Toronto, Canada	124 miles
Erie, PA	71 miles		

LOCATION OF BRADFORD, MCKEAN COUNTY, PENNSYLVANIA

The Bradford Pressed Brick Company Band, 1917. The band played regularly in the annual St. Rocco's Day festival in Bradford. Posed here in front of the brick company's office in Lewis Run are company owner William Hanley (at far left, second row). The band members include Barb Costanza, Santo Valenti, Tony Piscitelli, Mike Langianese, Jim Piscitelli, Lib Monago, Pete Monago, Mike Thomas, Carl Pietranton, Carm Vigilotti, John Romano, Clem Piscitelli, Frank Pietranton, Pete Tompetti, Ray Haven, Don Monago, Mr. Zanelli, Lib Costanzo, Ben Iaderosa, and Val Vomola.

THE BRADFORD PRESSED BRICK COMPANY BAND OF 1917
BAND MEMBERS INCLUDED PISCITELLI FAMILY MEMBERS—
JIM PISCITELLI, CLEM PISCITELLI, AND BARB COSTANZO.

ST. BERNARD'S SCHOOL 1904

ST. BERNARD HIGH SCHOOL FOOTBALL LETTERMEN 1939
FRONT ROW: JIM NUNNAMAKER. BACK ROW: LEFT
TO RIGHT: GEORGE CORIGNANI, PETE DEPALMA,
PAUL SHIELDS, NICK CAMAS, NAZ PISCITELLI

ST. BERNARD HIGH SCHOOL CLASS OF 1939.
NAZ IS IN THE TOP ROW, 4TH FROM THE LEFT.
SOURCE: JIM GREGO, CLASS OF 1939, TOP ROW, 5TH FROM THE
RIGHT. THERE WERE 39 GRADUATES IN THE CLASS OF '39.

NAT AND HIS MOTHER, ANNA PISCITELLI, 1942

NAT AND FRAN IN LOUISVILLE, KY, FEBRUARY 25, 1943

POSTCARD FROM PVT. MIKE LANGIANESE, JR. TO ALBERT
COSTANZO FROM CAMP HOOD, TEXAS, AUGUST 16, 1943

POSTCARD FROM PVT. MIKE LANGIANESE, JR. TO
"BARB" FROM THE ARMY RECEPTION CENTER,
NEW CUMBERLAND, PA, AUGUST 4, 1943

NAT AND FRAN'S WEDDING DAY, AUGUST 21, 1943

A TRIP TO LEWIS RUN
LEFT TO RIGHT: FRANCES BURGY (FRAN'S MOTHER),
FRAN, PEGGY ANNE, GRANDMA ANNA PISCITELLI
OCTOBER 1944

AT CLUB MADRID IN LOUISVILLE, KY, APRIL 1945
LEFT TO RIGHT: FAYE PISCITELLI (WIFE OF JAMES PISCITELLI),
FRANCES (WIFE OF NAT), CLEM PISCITELLI, VERA PISCITELLI

NAT'S BROTHERS, FRANK PISCITELLI AND CLEM PISCITELLI

NAT AND HIS M4 SHERMAN TANK

NAT'S FATHER, HUMBERT PISCITELLI,
OUTSIDE HIS HOME IN LEWIS RUN, PA, 1973

NAT'S MOTHER, ANNA PISCITELLI,
LEWIS RUN, PA, 1960

NAT'S PARENTS ON THEIR 50TH ANNIVERSARY
AUGUST 15, 1956
HUMBERT PISCITELLI AND ANNA CARRARA PISCITELLI

THE PISCITELLI BOYS
1981 PISCITELLI FAMILY REUNION
LEFT TO RIGHT: VINCENZO (JAMES), STEPHANO (STEVE),
FRANCESCO (FRANK), NATALINO (NAZ), CLEMENTE (CLEM)

THE PISCITELLI GIRLS
1981 PISCITELLI FAMILY REUNION
LEFT TO RIGHT: FILOMENA (FANNIE), VINCENZA
(VINCIE), VIRGINIA, ANTOINETTE (TONET),
ELVERA (VERA), LOUISA (LOUISE)

NAT AT HIS 50TH CLASS REUNION IN 1989
BRADFORD, PA
SOURCE: JIM GREGO, CLASS OF 1939

NAT AND FRAN
SEPTEMBER 19, 1992
AT THEIR GRANDSON'S WEDDING
(PEGGY ANNE'S OLDEST SON, STEVEN)

XII. WORLD WAR II SERVICE MEMBERS

(134) LEWIS RUN, PA

—

ALPHABETICAL LISTING

KEY:
Army and Army Air Corps (106)
(M) Marine Corps (4)
(N) Navy (24)
 Served Overseas (97)

STATISTICS:
Killed—7
Wounded—4
Prisoner of War—1
Missing in Action—1

Atkinson, Kenneth (A)*
Bagnato, Jim (A)
Bagnato, Mike (A)*
Bagnato, Rocco (A)
Benedict, Frank (A)
Benedict, Rose (A) (Nurse)
Bombasay, Deno (A)*
Breese, Floyd (A)
Case, Douglas (N)

Chochrach, Paul (N)*

Chochrach, Steve (A) (Presumed dead when his B-25 bomber
was lost over the Atlantic Ocean in March 1942 while
hunting German Submarines (U-Boats))

Costanzo, Albert (A) (Made the Army his career)

Costanzo, Carl (N) (Made the Navy his career)

Curcio, John (A) (Killed in a training accident in Texas)

Curcio, Paul (A)

DeFillippo, John (A) (Killed in action in France on June 25, 1944)

DelMonago, Mario (A)*

DelMonago, Benito (A)*

Delvecchio, Joe (A)

DePrater, Raymond (N)*

DePrater, Richard (N)* (Killed at sea in the Pacific)

DePrater, Robert (A)* (Missing in action in the Pacific)

DePrater, Victor (N)*

DePrater, Walter (N)*

DePrater, Wesley (N)*

DiBiase, John (A)*

DiFonzo, Paul (A)*

DiFonzo, Frank (A)*

Dorguzzi, Esther (M)

Dorguzzi, Julius (A)*

Fair, Charlie (A)* (Killed in action in Europe)

Fair, Frank (A)*

Fair, Mike (A)*

Fair, "Red" (N)*

Foster, Albert (N)*

Foster, David (N)*

Foster, Robert (A)

Franco, Fino (A)*

Franco, Messino (A)*

Frigo, Dario (N)*

Frigo, Deno (A)*

Frigo, Leo (A)*

Giordano, Angelo (N)*

Giordano, Anthony (N)*

Giordano, Carmine (A)*

Giordano, Tony (A)*

Glenn, George (A)

Gordon, Edwin (A)* (Killed in action in Europe)

Huntoon, Frederick (N)* (Killed at sea in the Pacific)

Juniack, Louie (N)*

Keane, Joe (A)*

Kutchmire, John (A)*

Langianese, Anthony (A)

Langianese, Frank (A)*

Langianese, Matt (A)*

Langianese, Mike, Jr. (A)* (Wounded)

Langianese, Sam (A)*

Leone, Jimmy (M)*

Leone, Mike (A)

Manning, Bill (A)*

Manning, John (A)*

Monago, Johnny (A)* (Prisoner of War, captured in North
  Africa in 1942, released in Germany in 1945)
Montecalvo, Albert (N)*
Montecalvo, James, Jr. (A)*
Montecalvo, Josephine (A)* (Nurse)
Morrison, Jack (A)*
Murphy, Patsy (A)*
Ogden, Bruce (A)*
Onuffer, Andy (A)*
Onuffer, Joe (A)
Onuffer, Paul (A)*
Pace, Alexander (A)*
Pace, Dominic (A)
Pace, Frank (N)
Pace, Guy (A)*
Pace, Rocco (A)*
Pais, Caesar (A)* (Wounded)
Pais, Sylvio (N)
Pantuso, Alley (A)*
Pantuso, Andy (A)*
Pantuso, Johnny (A)*
Pantuso, Louis (N)
Pantuso, Vincent (M)*
Pelino, Tony (A)*
Perrini, Sylvio (A)* (Wounded)
Perry, Hallis (A)*
Pingie, Alfred (A)*

Pingie, John (A)*

Pingie, Nat (A)

Piscitelli, Clemente (A)* (Served in Australia and New Guinea)

Piscitelli, Frank (A) (Was drafted with only one eye)

Piscitelli, Nat (A)* (Wounded in the Battle of the Bulge on January 4, 1945. Lost one eye but returned to his unit in Germany after three months in a hospital in England)

Raffele, Frank (A)*

Rose, Frank (A)*

Rose, Mike, Jr. (N)*

Ross, Anthony (A)*

Ross, James (A)

Ross, Joseph, Jr. (A)* (Gunner on a B-17 bomber in England from December 1944 to March 1945 where he flew 36 combat missions)

Ross, Michael ("Friday") (A)

Royer, Cecil (A)*

Sankner, George (M)*

Sankner, Joe (A)*

Sankner, Steve, Jr. (A)*

Shaffner, Roy, Jr. (N)*

Sloppy, Ben (A)*

Sloppy, Francis (A)*

Sloppy, Harrison (A)*

Smith Robert (A)

Spencer, Richard (N)*

Susi, Alfred (A)

Susi, Angelo, (A)*
Susi, Dan (A)*
Susi, Humbert (A)*
Sweeney, Burl (A)*
Tanty, Phil (A)*
Tasin, Rocky, (A)
Tasin, Leo (A)
Torrey, Robert (N)
Vecellio, Chuck (A)
Vecellio, Henry (A)*
Vecellio, Jimmy (A)
Vecellio, Mac (A)
Vecellio, Robert (A)*
Vecellio, Valentino, (A)*
Ventura, Joe (A)*
Vinca, Pete (A)*
Wozer, John, Jr. (A)* (P-47 Thunderbolt pilot in Europe)
Zamberlan, Peo (A)*
Zandi, Aldo (A)*
Zandi, Carl (A)*
Zandi, Ettore (A)*
Zandi, Louie (A)*
Zandi, Paul (A)
Zandi, Tony (A)

This list obtained from Fannie Ross, Nat's oldest sister

www.ingramcontent.com/pod-product-compliance
Lightning Source LLC
Chambersburg PA
CBHW021126020426
42331CB00005B/641